Pressure Point

Other Books by Scott Renyard

Illustrated Screenplays

Who Killed Miracle? (2022)

The Pristine Coast (2023)

The Unofficial Trial of Alexandra Morton (2023)

The Herring People (2023)

Trial of an Iconic Species (2023)

Children's Books

The Flag That Flew Up (2021)

PRESSURE POINT
a series of mishandled events

Scott Renyard

juggernaut CLASSICS

Pressure Point: A series of mishandled events
Copyright © 2024 Scott Renyard

TV series copyright: 2023 Pacific Coast Entertainment Ltd.

All rights reserved.

No part of this publication may be reproduced or transmitted in any form or by any means, electronic or mechanical, including photocopying, recording or by any information storage and retrieval system, now known or to be invented, without permission in writing from the publisher.

This book and the television series it is based on are works of fiction. While they were inspired by events and situations in the real world, the characters and situations they portray are products of the creator's imagination.

Published by Juggernaut Classics Inc.
Contact: scott@juggernautpictures.ca

ISBN: 978-1-998836-58-1 (softcover)

Edited by Lesley Cameron

Cover design by Caid Dow and Jan Westendorp
Book design by Jan Westendorp/katodesignandphoto.com

Juggernaut Classics Inc.

Contents

INTRODUCTION	vii
Pressure Point: A series of mishandled events	1
CAST OF CHARACTERS	3
Episode 1: Dumbing Down the Database	7
Episode 2: Mine Your Own Business	43
Episode 3: The Great Escape	84
Episode 4: Fishy Oil Slick	121
Episode 5: Nothing but Pipeline Dreams	158
Episode 6: The Fine Art of Sustainable Clear-Cuts	190
Episode 7: The Poop Dilution Solution	229
Episode 8: The Benefits of Surplus Killer Whales	263
Episode 9: Climate Change Is a Good Thing	297
Episode 10: Evasive Techniques 101	330
ACKNOWLEDGEMENTS	367

Introduction

Several years ago I was on a brief film shoot in Calgary. My flight back to Vancouver was delayed due to bad weather, so I went into a restaurant to grab something to eat. While I ate, I watched a news program on one of the restaurant's television screens. One of the news items was about an oil spill, and it included an impromptu interview with a politician trying to explain away the lack of response to the spill. I found myself thinking about the many statements made over the years by politicians in response to environmental disasters. Their statements were often vague descriptions of what had happened and what they would change so it didn't happen again. But more often than not, the environmental disasters not only happened again but happened over and over again. I wondered what the politicians were actually thinking when they were trying to explain why something had happened and what they were going to do about it. And I wondered if they wished they could say what they were really thinking. With that thought, a comedic format came to me and *Pressure Point* was born.

I pulled out my laptop, and within about three hours I had written rough drafts for nine episodes of a comedy interview series. This is not how the writing process usually goes for me, because the serious documentaries I create often require many months of intensive research, interviews, and painstaking filming. But in this case, I only needed a basic knowledge of pressing environmental issues or events to weave them into a series of cheeky mock interviews. In a sentence, it was fun and liberating to just weave together the random thoughts and ideas about the environmental ethos that were floating around in my brain. I hope you find them enlightening—and most of all, entertaining.

Episode 1 was inspired by the Harper government's closing of 25 libraries on June 12, 2012. The closure process included consolidating 11 Department of Fisheries and Oceans (DFO) libraries into four. Popular opinion about these events was that the government's so-called cost-cutting actions were really a move to eliminate a knowledge base that could impede the development of natural resources—and in particular, oil and gas. I thought it would be fun to explore how the loss of these libraries, and the knowledge they contained, might affect the commercial interests of certain businesses, especially when those businesses might not realize that the resources they wanted to cash in on—like certain fish species, for example—might need non-commercial inputs like bugs.

Episode 2 was inspired by the Mount Polley mine disaster on August 4, 2014. An entire watershed was wiped out when a tailings pond dam burst, releasing 25 billion litres of contaminated mining waste into Polley Lake, Hazeltine Creek, Quesnel Lake, and the Cariboo River. It was determined that the dam failed because of a layer of glacial till under the tailings pond. In other words, a layer of faulty mud. There was much public puzzlement over why the mining company wasn't slapped with large fines, lawsuits, or even jail time. After all, this was one of the largest mining disasters ever. I got to thinking that the company was likely complying with the terms of its permit and so government regulators were probably at least partially to blame for the disaster. I wondered how a politician might explain the lack of accountability for one of the largest mining disasters our planet has ever suffered.

Episode 3 was inspired by a series of reports about large numbers of farm fish escapees from open net pen fish farms. In 1989, 390,000 chinook escaped from a BC fish farm in just one event. Then, in

1997, 360,000 Atlantic salmon escaped from a Washington State fish farm. And in 2000, 350,000 farm fish escaped when a storm destroyed a fish farm. These are large, arguably unusual, events, but smaller-scale fish farm escapes are a regular occurrence because small tears in the nets allow a certain percentage of the stock to escape before the mature fish are harvested. Over the years, many politicians have rushed to the defence of open net fish farm operators and downplayed the problem. One BC provincial politician even once claimed that only two fish had ever escaped from BC fish farms in all the years the farms had been in operation. This incredible claim got me thinking that there were likely even more outlandish claims that could be made about how Atlantic salmon came to be on the Pacific coast. For example, what if Atlantic salmon were actually fish tourists looking for juvenile Pacific salmon to mate with?

Episode 4 was inspired by the events of June 14, 2015, when Vancouver area residents woke to the news that a clean-up of a 5,000-litre diesel oil spill was underway in False Creek at Fisherman's Wharf. Witnesses to the oil spill saw a full emergency response that included the Canadian coast guard, local police, the Vancouver fire department, and even ambulances. This oil spill response presented a stark contrast to the response to the 2,700-litre bunker oil spill that occurred just three months earlier in Burrard Inlet near Stanley Park. The public was outraged at the lack of response to the earlier spill, and most of the wrath focused on the environmental cutbacks made by the federal government. I thought the timing of the False Creek disaster was quite fortuitous for the government, given that it was just a few months away from the October 19, 2015, election. I guess you don't always associate good fortune with oil spills, but clearly this one gave the government a golden opportunity to fix a glaring problem right before the election. How lucky was that? But it might not have been luck at all. I was in the area with my camera on the morning of the clean-up, gathering footage for my documentary *The Herring People*. As I was walking back to my car with the camera in tow, I ran into one of the officials involved in the clean-up. He pointed me toward where the press conference would be. On the off-chance that something would come out of it that would help my film, I wandered over. But the press conference seemed to me to be about what a great job the government was doing to protect the environment from oil spills and how it had fixed the response to spills. When I asked a question about whether any of the clean-up crews had identified any impact on the juvenile fish using the bay, the spokesperson quickly said there was no impact on the fish. How could they be so sure of that after only a few hours of clean-up? After the conference was over, I ran into one of my subjects for *The Herring People* and he told me that the locals had told him they thought the spill was not an accident but a deliberate spill. I was flabbergasted. I asked around, and other people corroborated the first local's story. Could it be that this spill was a set-up to show that the lack of response to oil spills had been fixed? In other words, was it possible that the False Creek spill was intended to boost the image of the government prior to the upcoming election? Without more evidence, we can't know for sure. However, this scenario seemed perfect for an episode showing what the comical response might have been had the word gotten out to journalists prior to the press conference.

Episode 5 was inspired by the 35 interveners who dropped out of the National Energy Board's review of the Trans Mountain pipeline expansion project. They complained that the hearings were unbalanced and biased and that they were only invited to add a veneer of legitimacy to them. The CBC reported that Robyn Allan, an economist, stepped back from what she saw as a "rigged" process, and the former BC Hydro president and CEO Marc Eliesen called the process a "farce."[1] I wondered how an interview would go if the politician in charge didn't have a

---

1   See https://www.cbc.ca/news/canada/british-columbia/kinder-morgan-pipeline-review-by-neb-loses-35-participants-over-flawed-process-1.3189123

good filter for his inside voice and answered questions as if they were multiple choice options in a survey where the questions are phrased in a way to elicit specific responses to support the green lighting of the project.

Episode 6 was inspired by the many times I saw a governing party assigning responsibility for more than one ministry to a key member of their caucus. Often a premier of a province or prime minister of Canada does this because the politician picked is reliable and rarely screws up. But I remember wondering on a few occasions how on earth a particular person would be able to run two or more ministries when the goals and mandates of those ministries were so different. Would the mandates of those ministries be equally promoted and heard in committees, or would the goals of one be reduced to ambient noise? I thought it might be interesting to interview a politician who is serving one ministry—whose mandate reflects his personal bias—with vigour and the other—whose mandate is less interesting to him—with nothing more than lip service. This was the result.

Episode 7 was inspired by the fact that for over 125 years, the city of Victoria, British Columbia, dumped raw sewage into the ocean. Finally, in January 2021, a new sewage treatment plant opened and began processing sewage from five municipalities in the Greater Victoria area. The Washington State governor congratulated the Premier of British Columbia for finally treating Victoria's sewage and reducing the impact on the Strait of Juan de Fuca, which we share with our American neighbours. Victoria even had its own mascot, Mr. Floatie, who protested for years about Victoria's raw sewage appearing on local beaches. After the plant opened, one writer reported that a few floaties had been found on a Victoria beach. It was suggested that these stray floaties were from some regions around Victoria that were not yet tied into the new sewage treatment plant. I thought there might be some creative ways for a politician to explain away this unfortunate issue with what most would consider to be a good news story for the marine environment off the southern tip of Vancouver Island. How did the rogue floaties really get onto the beach? What if the minister responsible was a conspiracy theorist who thinks that the floaties could be a result of illegal immigration or a symptom of the on-again, off-again log dispute between Canada and the United States? Or what if something even more sinister was at play?

Episode 8 was inspired by a news report that the endangered Southern Resident Killer Whale darlings of British Columbia's coast were starving and that their population numbers were in a spiral of decline. A lot of ink has been devoted to covering this small population, and any births or deaths instantly become headline news in British Columbia. Between 2012 and 2020, the Southern Resident Killer Whale population had 17 births, and six of those newborns went missing or died at some point. During the same period, 26 adults went missing or died. So, the average annual birth rate of this population is less than two and deaths of adults in this population have been slightly more than the birth rate. These statistics suggest that the population is slowly going extinct. There has been much speculation about the cause of the decline of this population. Some experts believe it's related to the lack of chinook salmon, the Southern Resident Killer whale's main food source. Others believe boat traffic and harassment from whale watching or contamination from oil spills and strikes from large ships are to blame. Maybe the decline is related to a combination of these factors. Every once in a while there is a huge cheer when a new Southern Resident offspring is seen swimming in the Salish Sea. I wondered what a business-minded government would do if suddenly there were a lot of births in this population in one year? Would they change their position on protecting them? And what steps might they take to celebrate the influx of new members of this small and endangered whale population?

Episode 9 was inspired by the daily onslaught of news reports about global warming and climate change. This is undeniably the most important environmental issue of our era, so it wouldn't be right to have a series of discussions with our fictional politicians about environmental issues without including this keystone topic. The issue is vast, and I wanted to bring it down to Earth—Flat Earth, in fact—and take the discussion from there. And what better way to poke a little fun at such a serious issue than to have a prime minister who believes that Earth is flat and that hot weather is an economic opportunity? After all, many governments around the world are eyeing easier access to the resources at both the North and South Poles as a huge opportunity as the ice melts away. So there must be other economic benefits to a warming planet, right?

Episode 10 came to me as I was driving down the road one day, listening to the radio. I noticed that a number of politicians were avoiding most of the discussion around their particular hot potato issue by using the vagaries of privacy laws, or a court proceeding, or some other legal pretext. I remember listening back in 2015 to an interview on CBC with Lorne Sossin, who was dean of the Osgoode Hall Law School at the time, in which he was asked about the "before the courts" excuse used by some politicians. He responded that many journalists accepted the excuse at face value and dropped the issue or line of questioning. The rule politicians were leaning on is called the sub judice rule. It exists to prevent governments from imposing undue influence on the outcome of a court proceeding. We can all see the benefits of politicians not being allowed to try to influence a court proceeding, but this rule is overused and abused by governments of all tendencies. I thought it might be fun to take it to an extreme and interview a politician who can talk about almost nothing because if it's not currently before the courts, it might be at some point in the future.

The original scripts became this book and the television series. They are intended to shine light on environmental issues past and present in a fun and exaggerated way. Politicians have a tough job—and some make it tougher than it needs to be. I think the public would like to hear more candid answers to questions about environmental issues, but our governments are so wedded to business interests that sometimes the self-imposed censorship becomes almost unbearable. I hope a glimpse into the minds of fictitious politicians with hard-to-control inside voices will allow us all to laugh a little about some of our more awful environmental performances in recent years. And who knows, maybe one day politicians will routinely lay bare their thoughts and biases and let us know what they really think.

Pressure Point:
A series of mishandled events

Written and Directed
by
Scott Renyard

Cast of Characters

PATRICK MALIHA plays Francis von Zoofendorfen, the host for the first season of the show *Pressure Point: A series of mishandled events.*

BRADLEY DUFFY plays an on-camera reporter for the show *Pressure Point: A series of mishandled events*.

GRACE CHIN plays an on-camera reporter for the show *Pressure Point: A series of mishandled events*.

KATHERINE BRANSGROVE plays an on-camera reporter for the show *Pressure Point: A series of mishandled events*.

Kyle Toy plays an on-camera reporter for the show *Pressure Point: A series of mishandled events.*

PATRICIA SIMS plays an on-camera reporter for the show *Pressure Point: A series of mishandled events.*

SHAYAN BAYAT plays an on-camera reporter for the show *Pressure Point: A series of mishandled events.*

EPISODE 1:

Dumbing Down the Database

David C. Jones plays Craig Crabtree, the Minister of Fisheries, aka the Minister of Fishy Data Suppression.

FADE IN:

                    ANNOUNCER
          Warning. Hyper-sensitive,
          serious and easily offended
          viewers and politicians may
          find that some dialogue will
          make them laugh. Consult your
          physician before consuming this
          content.

AUDIO STATIC, TV COLOUR BARS SPAGHETTI AND DISAPPEAR

EXT. VANCOUVER CITY (AERIAL) — NIGHT

A brilliant shot of the downtown core all lit up.

                    VON ZOOFENDORFEN
          It's time for *Pressure Point*.
          Here's what people have been
          watching and hearing in the
          news this week.

INT. MODERN BAR — DAY

A TV hangs from the ceiling. On the screen there is an image of yellow tape that reads "POLICE LINE DO NOT CROSS." An anxious reporter is reporting his story in an urgent tone of voice.

                    REPORTER 1
               Police are investigating a
               report by . . .

EXT. DEPARTMENT OF FISHERIES VANCOUVER
BUILDING — DAY

The reflection of the Canadian flag stretches
across many stories of the skyscraper.

                    REPORTER 1
                 . . . a former DFO employee
               that the PMO acted beyond . . .

The word "Canada" at the top of the building
marks it as a government building.

                    REPORTER 1
                 . . . its powers by destroying
               public databases.

INT. GREENHOUSE — DAY

A cellphone is leaning against a spool of
garden twine. A news story playing on the
phone pans the Vancouver Law Courts building.

                    REPORTER 2
               A former DFO librarian is
               taking her former employer, the
               Federal Government, to court
               today.

ON A DOCUMENT

It's the Federal Government order about the downsizing of the DFO library system.

>   REPORTER 2
>   But it's not over wrongful
>   dismissal. Instead, she
>   contends that the Government,
>   in closing down its
>   libraries . . .

INT. PRINTING SHOP — DAY

A photo of a dumpster half-full of a bunch of documents.

>   REPORTER 2
>   . . . was committing a crime by
>   destroying public property.

AUDIO STATIC, TV COLOUR BARS SPAGHETTI AND DISAPPEAR

INT. MODERN BAR — DAY

ANOTHER TV — hanging from the ceiling.

A news report features a photo of the Canadian Parliament building.

                    REPORTER 1
               The PMO responded by saying
               that . . .

The image is replaced by one of an office
floor. There is nothing in the office but
empty desks.

                    REPORTER 1
               . . . it was perfectly within
               its mandate . . .

EXT. RECYCLING CENTRE — DAY

Stacks of office equipment and computers.

                    REPORTER 1
               . . . to streamline government
               operations . . .

EXT. AVERAGE BAR — DAY

A TV hangs on the wall. The news report shows
an Experimental Lake.

                    REPORTER 1
               . . . and use surplus public
               assets to fill in the
               Experimental Lakes . . .

ANOTHER ANGLE — tighter on the lake.

>   REPORTER 1
>   . . . which had also become
>   expendable.

AUDIO STATIC, TV COLOUR BARS SPAGHETTI AND DISAPPEAR

INT. WORKSHOP — DAY

A radio sits next to a radial arm saw.

PUSHING IN — on the news report blaring from the radio.

>   REPORTER 3
>   The Government continued its
>   assault on Canadian scientists
>   today by closing yet another
>   research facility. It's
>   clear muzzling scientists is
>   spreading right across the
>   country.

AUDIO STATIC, TV COLOUR BARS SPAGHETTI AND DISAPPEAR

INT. LIVING ROOM — DAY

A TV sits on an entertainment stand. A reporter, Bradley Duffy, is reporting for Channel Therlve news.

                    REPORTER 4
          Scientists have taken to
          the streets today in protest
          against the Government's
          move to muzzle them. They
          complain that the muzzles are
          a violation of their Charter
          of Rights and Freedoms and
          unfairly target their sexual
          kinks.

The report goes live to a greenhouse where
muzzled scientists are waving signs in
protest.

                    REPORTER 4
          One bureaucrat I spoke with
          said, "That's the point.

ANOTHER ANGLE — the scientists march close to
the cameraman.

                    REPORTER 4
          We want the sexual orientation
          of . . .

BACK TO REPORTER 4

                    REPORTER 4
          . . . scientists to be out in
          the public so that people know
          the Government employs people
                       (MORE)

                    REPORTER 4 (CONT'D)
               of all sexual orientations in
               the public service."

INT. BURGER SHACK — DAY

A TV hangs on the wall. Another news reporter, this one for Non Cents News, is on location at the protest.

ANOTHER TV

A different camera crew is filming the protests.

                         REPORTER 5
               One criticism lodged against
               scientists is that they are, as
               a group, logical and rational
               to the point of being boring.
               Well, today scientists shot
               back, saying that their kink
               is underappreciated and that
               they actually prefer whips and
               chains to the now government-
               mandated muzzles.

INT. RESTAURANT — MOMENTS LATER

A TV is high on the wall. A reporter continues his report.

                    REPORTER 4
          The scientists say, however,
          that the Government is all
          about silencing the public
          release of their research if
          not their sexual orientation,
          and isn't that what we were
          talking about? The Government
          has said that is patently
          untrue.

INT. AUTO REPAIR OFFICE — DAY

Reporter 4 is visible on the monitor of a desktop computer.

                    REPORTER 4
          And they just want to show
          their support for the S and
          M tendencies of scientists
          everywhere as an under-
          represented and repressed
          group. Repressed, of course,
          by the Government.

INT. WAITING ROOM — DAY

The Channel Therlve news report is playing at this establishment as well.

                    REPORTER 4
          The official added that
          scientists can finally show
          their sexual orientation and
          no longer have to hide their
          S and M tendencies behind
          closed laboratory doors. And
          the Government has since
          mandated muzzles for scientists
          everywhere.

AUDIO STATIC, TV COLOUR BARS SPAGHETTI AND
DISAPPEAR

INTRO ANIMATION

A slick graphic blends images and geometric
shapes, then wraps around to reveal the
title: *Pressure Point*.

AUDIO STATIC, TV COLOUR BARS SPAGHETTI AND
DISAPPEAR

INT. PRESSURE POINT STUDIO — DAY

Our host, Francis von Zoofendorfen, looks
into camera.

                    VON ZOOFENDORFEN
          Hello and welcome to *Pressure
          Point*. I'm your host, Francis
          von Zoofendorfen. And joining
                    (MORE)

                    VON ZOOFENDORFEN (CONT'D)
               me today, we have none other
               than the Minister of Fisheries
               and Oceans, Craig Crabtree.

He swivels his chair to look at his guest.

                    VON ZOOFENDORFEN
               Welcome to the show, Mr.
               Crabtree.

ON CRABTREE — wearing glasses and looking slightly nervous.

                    CRABTREE
               Thanks for having me.

BACK TO VON ZOOFENDORFEN

                    VON ZOOFENDORFEN
               Well, normally, Minister, we
               would focus on fishing quotas,
               openings and whether the
               harvest rate is sustainable
               etc., etc.—

WIDER — Crabtree looks at his notes.

                    CRABTREE
               —Yes. Yes, that's the usual—

INTERCUT — between the two.

                    VON ZOOFENDORFEN
          —But the recent move made by
          the Government to downsize
          your ministry's libraries has
          been said by many to be, and I
          quote, "a rather archaic move."

Crabtree nervously puts his hand to his
mouth.

                    CRABTREE
          Yes. We, we did archive some
          documents.

                    VON ZOOFENDORFEN
          No. Archaic. As in, your
          move to close and dispose of
          a lot of books and data has
          been compared to the old book
          burnings. . . . Ah, tell me,
          how do you respond to those
          comparisons?

More nervous gestures.

                    CRABTREE
          I hate them. I hate it. It's,
          it's just a bunch of, ah, left-
          leaning fish huggers that have
          never had to pay any bills.

                    VON ZOOFENDORFEN
          But, ok, Minister. There were
          decades of data stored at those
          facilities. So, where did it
          all go?

                    CRABTREE
          Well, the good stuff we kept
          and, or digitized.

                    VON ZOOFENDORFEN
          Oh, ok. So where is that going
          to go or be?

                    CRABTREE
          The good stuff will be put
          online, ah, eventually.

Crabtree looks down at his notes.

                    CRABTREE
          And, ah, the rest. Well. Well.
          WELL. We, we, we, we, ah, need
          to make sure that the citizens
          are getting good value for
          their money. And, and storing
          a bunch of, ah, useless
          information. . . . is, ah,
          well, useless. And a waste of
          taxpayers' money.

VON ZOOFENDORFEN
Ok. So you feel that deleting the databases is going to save taxpayers' money?

CRABTREE
It's just a bunch of numbers, and you know what they say about facts and statistics.

VON ZOOFENDORFEN
What? What do they say?

CRABTREE
It doesn't add up. It's all just a bunch of gobbly goop.

VON ZOOFENDORFEN
Gobbly goop. Am I to understand correctly that you feel that databases are not important?

CRABTREE
Well, it's not that I don't think that they are important. It just slows down the decision-making process and wastes a lot of precious time.

VON ZOOFENDORFEN
So, you are saying that it's inconvenient to the political process.

Crabtree points at von Zoofendorfen, flexing his index finger in and out, then points at himself.

CRABTREE
You could say that, you could say that. I won't say that.

VON ZOOFENDORFEN
Ok, then, how about this? How many people relied on that information?

CRABTREE
Just a few staff members. Not many more.

VON ZOOFENDORFEN
Were the libraries open to the public?

CRABTREE
No. No. No. No. No. Why, why would we do that? Terrible idea. People need not look at what they need not see.

                    VON ZOOFENDORFEN
Ok, well, do you think that
they didn't look because of
the fact that none of them
were available or open to the
general public? Do you think
that might have been the reason
no one used them?

                    CRABTREE
It might have. But if someone
really insisted, they could
have made an appointment.

                    VON ZOOFENDORFEN
Ok. Let me ask you this. What
if a researcher came along one
day and saw something in our
Canadian historical data set
and discovered something that
could be of great benefit to
the public?

                    CRABTREE
Oh, well, that's, ha, ha, ha,
not likely to happen. That
is an unlikely probability.
An unlikely possibility. A
plausible possibility. Yes.
YESSS!

VON ZOOFENDORFEN
So, a possibility.

Crabtree raises his hands and does the separating thumb trick.

CRABTREE
Well, anything is possible. Even the impossible is possible.

VON ZOOFENDORFEN
Ok, well, nicely put.

CRABTREE
Thanks. Thanks. Certainties are better, but I'm pretty sure that nobody would find anything that is usable in those useless data sets at all. Ah, it would be totally useless.

VON ZOOFENDORFEN
Ah, ok. Well, thank you for clearing that up!

They both laugh uncontrollably. Von Zoofendorfen suddenly stops.

VON ZOOFENDORFEN
Let's turn to your government's move to gut section 35 of the *Fisheries Act*.

CRABTREE
Yes, one of the best moves our federal government has made so far, don't you think?

VON ZOOFENDORFEN
You, you really think so?

CRABTREE
Well, yes, yes, those sections were protecting all fish, of all types, for all reasons. They were just getting in the way of everything else. They were just not practical. Nope, not at all practical.

VON ZOOFENDORFEN
Ok, but what it did do was provide a sober second thought for any project so that we didn't cause irreparable harm to our fish populations.

CRABTREE
Hmmph. All fish are not created equal.

                    VON ZOOFENDORFEN
               Really?

Crabtree picks up a poster-sized card from
the floor.

                    CRABTREE
               Hmmm. Of course.

ON A POSTER — of cartoon-like drawings of
fish. They are painted in bright, pretty
colours.

                    CRABTREE
               There are some useful
               commercial species and the
               rest . . .

He pulls the first poster away to reveal
a second poster with more cartoon-like
drawings. These ones are coloured black and
brown.

                    CRABTREE
               . . . are just fish.

Crabtree ducks around the side of the poster.

                    CRABTREE
               Useless fish.

                        VON ZOOFENDORFEN
                   Useless fish. What are useless
                   fish?

Crabtree is checking his notes on index
cards.

WIDER — Crabtree holds up both cards side-
by-side.

                        VON ZOOFENDORFEN
                   These are Useful fish and . . .

BACK TO THE POSTERS

                             CRABTREE
                   . . . these are Useless fish.

                        VON ZOOFENDORFEN
                   Useless fish. Wow. Ok, it's
                   like, it's like watching a
                   cartoon but much, much slower.

Crabtree is now hunched over in the chair
like he's having a crisis.

                        VON ZOOFENDORFEN
                   Ok, I'm going to get back on
                   track. I'm going to ask you a
                   very poignant question. And if
                   you don't have flash cards for
                             (MORE)

VON ZOOFENDORFEN (CONT'D)
this one, that's ok. What
you're saying to me, if I
understand correctly, is that
if a species has no commercial
value, then it's not worth
protecting?

CRABTREE
Precisely.

VON ZOOFENDORFEN
Ok, well, and who determines
what has value and what does
not?

CRABTREE
I do.

VON ZOOFENDORFEN
You do?

CRABTREE
Yes, I do. In consultation with
the Prime Minister, of course.
Right. Ah, ah, but it's not
complicated. If humans do not
eat a type of fish, then it's
pretty much, ah, pretty much,

He shows the "Useless" card again and then
looks at his notes.

                    CRABTREE
          . . . a Useless fish.

                VON ZOOFENDORFEN
          With no exceptions?

                    CRABTREE
          Well, I suppose if, ah, ah, ah,
          if there was a species like,
          like, for example, the, the
          pink salmon—

                VON ZOOFENDORFEN
          —The pink salmon.

                    CRABTREE
          That fish is used in pet food.

                VON ZOOFENDORFEN
          Ok.

Crabtree thinks for a second.

                    CRABTREE
          Yes, yes, yes, if there is
          a fish, ah, ah, species like
          that, that could still be
          seen as commercial. Then, yes,
          I would say that is a type
          of fish that we could, ah,
          protect. Um, yes, it doesn't
                      (MORE)

>   CRABTREE (CONT'D)
> always have to be ah, ah, a
> fish humans eat. Ah, yes, as
> long as it makes money. That's
> the key. Money.

He puts the index card down.

ON VON ZOOFENDORFEN

>   VON ZOOFENDORFEN
> Money is the key. Why am I not
> surprised?

>   CRABTREE
> Yes, money. That's it.

>   VON ZOOFENDORFEN
> Ok. What about this?

TIGHTER

>   VON ZOOFENDORFEN
> What if one of your commercial
> species preys on another
> species that we don't eat or
> use for something? Now, is that
> species worth saving?

> CRABTREE
> I would say probably not. And I wouldn't stop an oil pipeline over something as marginal as that. Right. Ah, ah. No. No. No. Commercial fish, in our humble opinion, do not have to eat non-commercial fish.

ON VON ZOOFENDORFEN — looking perplexed.

BACK TO — Crabtree.

> CRABTREE
> So the non-commercial fish would not need protection.

> VON ZOOFENDORFEN
> Ok, well, what would the commercially viable fish do, then, for food?

> CRABTREE
> They could eat bugs.

> VON ZOOFENDORFEN
> They could eat bugs?

ON VON ZOOFENDORFEN

                    VON ZOOFENDORFEN
          Ok, well, then . . . What if
          the bugs are also killed by the
          oil or the development?

ON CRABTREE

                    VON ZOOFENDORFEN (O.S.)
          Then what?

                    CRABTREE
          They could eat something else,
          of course. OH! OH! I can see
          what you are doing.

BACK TO VON ZOOFENDORFEN

                    VON ZOOFENDORFEN
          You can?

BACK TO CRABTREE

                    CRABTREE
          Yeah, yeah. You're gonna go
          right down the whole food, ah,
          chain to try to prove the point
          that everything is valuable.
          Well, hmm-hmm. That's not going
          to work with me, Buster Brown!

VON ZOOFENDORFEN (O.S.)
It's, it's not?

CRABTREE
No, no, no, it's not. They aren't going to go hungry, right! Ah, ah, the important fish are quite adaptable and they, they will figure it out. They will figure out what to eat.

Crabtree holds up one of his fish cards as if it has information on it.

VON ZOOFENDORFEN
And . . . Ok, where did you hear that?

Crabtree realizes he grabbed the wrong card. He reaches for another one and holds it up. It reads: "EXCESS OIL COMPANY — Environmental Protection Division." It looks like it was made by a child. He quickly puts it back on the floor.

CRABTREE
From the environmental protection division of the Excess Oil Company.

                    VON ZOOFENDORFEN
Oh, ok. Let me get this
straight. Could I see that sign
once again? You mean to tell
me, this company right here,
the Excess Oil Company, they
said that commercial fish would
adapt to other food sources and
they would figure it out?

                    CRABTREE
Well, I'm paraphrasing, of
course.

                    VON ZOOFENDORFEN
Ok.

                    CRABTREE
But it's all a very sound
assumption. Ah, fish, fish are
not fussy eaters, generally,
and they will just find
something else to eat. Ah, they
could eat sticks.

                    VON ZOOFENDORFEN
Oh my lord.

                    CRABTREE
Yes, he will help as well.

                    VON ZOOFENDORFEN
          Don't you feel it's easier
          to just simply protect the
          environment?

                    CRABTREE
          Good God, no. No, no, no, no.
          That's a crazy idea!!

                    VON ZOOFENDORFEN
          Really?

Crabtree nods.

                    VON ZOOFENDORFEN
          Well, ok . . . Don't you feel
          that these non-commercial
          species have a right to exist?

                    CRABTREE
          No. Ah. No. Not really. It's
          all just part of natural
          selection in the bigger
          picture.

                    VON ZOOFENDORFEN
          If you don't mind, explain to
          the audience what the bigger
          picture is?

CRABTREE
Well, if a fish population is so dumb—

VON ZOOFENDORFEN
—Ok—

CRABTREE
—as to specialize in a particular type of environment, right?

VON ZOOFENDORFEN
Yes.

CRABTREE
And, and that environment happens to be next to a, a, an important mine or an oil project. And if their habitat suddenly changes, right?

VON ZOOFENDORFEN
Ok.

CRABTREE
And they can't adapt quickly to the changing conditions.

VON ZOOFENDORFEN
Ok. I'm still following you.

CRABTREE
And, well . . . Um, well, well, it's not really our fault.

VON ZOOFENDORFEN
Ok.

CRABTREE
Right.

They are both squirming in their chairs, like they are trying to adapt to their environment, with von Zoofendorfen following Crabtree's lead, but not all that successfully.

VON ZOOFENDORFEN
Right.

CRABTREE
That we are more, more, more evolved and adaptable, and they are not more, more evolved or adaptable.

VON ZOOFENDORFEN
Hmm, hmm.

Crabtree is getting visibly more and more uncomfortable trying to explain his position.

                    CRABTREE
Um, yeah, it, it's, it's
ah . . . I mean, we can't be
the keepers for everyone and
everything. Right? Um, yeah,
it's not practical. It's part
of evolution. We shouldn't get
in the way of God's will now,
should we?

                    VON ZOOFENDORFEN
Ok, so you don't care if they
go extinct because of something
that we did to wipe them out?

                    CRABTREE
Well, we—

                    VON ZOOFENDORFEN
—Yes?—

                    CRABTREE
—do what we do to survive,
and they do what they do to
survive. Everyone does what
everyone does to survive. Ok?

                    VON ZOOFENDORFEN
I won't disagree with that.

                    CRABTREE
It's all really simple
actually. It's evolution in
action. Or not. Survival of the
fittest beats survival of the
less fittest.

                VON ZOOFENDORFEN
Survival of the fittest beats
survival of the less fittest.
That's not even a . . . Ok
then, how about this? And what
if all this habitat degradation
results in an environment
humans can't adapt to?

                    CRABTREE
Ha! Ha! Ha! Oh, oh, you're a
funny guy. Don't be ludicrous.
Oh, I thought this was supposed
to be a serious show.

Crabtree glances around, looking to see if
he's being pranked.

                VON ZOOFENDORFEN
    Ok.

ON VON ZOOFENDORFEN

                    VON ZOOFENDORFEN
          Well, I feel the need to tell
          you that question was actually
          sent in to us . . .

ON CRABTREE

                    VON ZOOFENDORFEN
          . . . by one of our viewers. A
          young lady, seven years of age,
          who . . .

BACK TO VON ZOOFENDORFEN

                    VON ZOOFENDORFEN
          We actually took her question
          because she has actually helped
          us with several graphics, or
          should I say flash cards. She
          said one of her dreams was to
          hand-colour something for her
          grandfather when he was on the
          show.

Von Zoofendorfen looks into camera. Then,

BACK TO CRABTREE — shocked.

                    VON ZOOFENDORFEN
          So that's uncomfortable for one
          of us.

Crabtree stands up.

> CRABTREE
> Whatever . . .

And he storms out.

> VON ZOOFENDORFEN
> Well, ok.

TIGHT ON VON ZOOFENDORFEN

> VON ZOOFENDORFEN
> Well, I guess that brings us to the end of our show. And there you have it. Not all fish are equal according to the Department of Fisheries and Oceans.

He looks into camera.

> VON ZOOFENDORFEN
> Once again, ladies and gentlemen, it has been interesting to say the least. I'm glad that you could join us, and as always I'm your host Francis von Zoofendorfen! And until next time, this has been *Pressure Point*.

>   CRABTREE (O.S.)
>   Did you really talk to my
>   granddaughter?

                              FADE TO:

EXT. VANCOUVER SKY (DRONE) — NIGHT

Fireworks explode into the night sky and we . . .

                              FADE OUT

EPISODE 2:

Mine Your Own Business

Graem Beddoes plays Mr. Stallward, the Minister of Mines and Resources, aka the Minister of Watershed Clean-Outs.

                    ANNOUNCER
          Warning. Hyper-sensitive,
          serious and easily offended
          viewers and politicians may
          find that some dialogue will
          make them laugh. Consult your
          physician before consuming this
          content.

AUDIO STATIC, TV COLOUR BARS SPAGHETTI AND
DISAPPEAR

EXT. VANCOUVER CITY (AERIAL) — NIGHT

A brilliant shot of the downtown core all
lit up.

                    VON ZOOFENDORFEN
          It's time for *Pressure Point*.
          Here's what people have been
          watching and hearing in the
          news this week.

INT. LIVING ROOM — DAY

A man is watching the news on his TV. A
reporter for BS Northwest News is standing
in front of a dam.

                    REPORTER 1
          A report from the Conservative
          Economic Institute concludes
          that regulation is getting in
          the way of deregulation.

INT. BEDROOM — MOMENTS LATER

A TV sits on a stand. The news is on.

                    REPORTER 1
          The report, penned by their own
          staff, says that government
          needs to set better regulations
          on deregulation so that new
          deregulated regulations ensure
          deregulation doesn't cause a
          loss of profitability in the
          private sector.

INT. SEWING SHOP — DAY

The report plays on a radio sitting on a
table.

                    REPORTER 1
          Some analysts say it all
          depends on your perspective
          as to whether it will work or
          not. Stay tuned for more on
          the regulation of deregulation
          saga.

AUDIO STATIC, TV COLOUR BARS SPAGHETTI AND DISAPPEAR

INT. REPAIR SHOP WAITING ROOM — DAY

The noon news is playing on a TV hung on the wall. A reporter is standing in an industrial area.

> REPORTER 2
> As one researcher put it, in a truly free market, businesses will undercut each other until everyone is offering their goods for free in order to get market share.

INT. CAFÉ — DAY

A radio sits on a box.

> REPORTER 3
> A left-leaning think tank today suggested that deregulation does not stimulate the economy as once predicted.

INT. LUMBER STORE — MOMENTS LATER

The report continues to blast from a radio hung on a beam.

                    REPORTER 3
          Instead, the experts say, it
          causes nothing but a narrowing
          of profits, takeovers by
          multinational corporations and
          a race to the bottom.

BACK TO REPORTER 2

                    REPORTER 2
          Maybe that's what they mean
          by a free market — where
          everything's free.

AUDIO STATIC, TV COLOUR BARS SPAGHETTI AND DISAPPEAR

INT. BEDROOM — DAY

Non Cents News is live on a small TV on the dresser.

Standing on the lawn of an industrial building, yet another reporter delivers news about a mining report.

                    REPORTER 4
          A mining survey report revealed
          that the return-on-investment
          or ROI on mining commodities is
          a poor performer.

INT. HOME OFFICE — MOMENTS LATER

The same reporter is visible on an iPad screen.

              REPORTER 4
     Over-estimated commodity
     prices, under-estimated capital
     costs, questionable management
     practices and . . .

INT. RESTAURANT — MOMENTS LATER

A small TV is perched high on a wall.

              REPORTER 4
     . . . over-inflated
     compensation packages make
     the sector one of the riskiest
     from a retail investment
     perspective.

INT. AUTOMOTIVE PARTS STORE — MOMENTS LATER

A TV is mounted on a makeshift shelf.

              REPORTER 4
     With profit margins
     historically slim, many
     companies are sacrificing
     safety for the sake of making
     a profit. And, as one writer
     said,

INT. OFFICE — MOMENTS LATER

The news is playing on the office computer.

>   REPORTER 4
>   . . . remediation of mining
>   sites is, well, basically out
>   of the question if you are to
>   have any profit at all. This
>   has been this week's mining
>   report and report on all things
>   related to economic pixie dust.

AUDIO STATIC, TV COLOUR BARS SPAGHETTI AND DISAPPEAR

A TV rests on a sideboard next to a purple vase. A raging flood is on the screen.

>   REPORTER 5
>   A tailings pond dam broke at
>   10:15 this morning,

AERIAL SHOT — of a tailings pond breach, with a massive mud flow taking out everything in its wake.

>   REPORTER 5
>   . . . sending a torrent of
>   debris . . .

ANOTHER SHOT — reveals the scale of the disaster.

                    REPORTER 5
               . . . and 25 million litres of
               contaminated mud . . .

INT. FOREST — MOMENTS LATER

The reporter stands in a pristine forest.

                    REPORTER 5
               . . . down a pristine watershed
               and into a salmon-bearing lake.

AUDIO STATIC, TV COLOUR BARS SPAGHETTI AND DISAPPEAR

INT. LIVING ROOM — MOMENTS LATER

ON A TV — the news is on and a reporter is at the Hope Slide, east of Hope, BC.

                    REPORTER 1
               A week ago, this slide was
               almost surpassed as the largest
               slide in British Columbia's
               history when a mine tailings
               pond burst, releasing 25
               million litres of mud and
               debris.

EXT. PATIO — MOMENTS LATER

Someone is watching the news on their iPad.

                    REPORTER 5
          Many questions surround the
          issue, like what happened and
          how could such a large dam have
          collapsed?

BACK TO LIVING ROOM

                    REPORTER 1
          The public is still waiting for
          answers.

INT. BEDROOM — MOMENTS LATER

TIGHT ON A TV SCREEN — perched in the corner on a dresser.

                    REPORTER 4
          Over to you.

INT. AUTOMOTIVE WAITING ROOM — MOMENTS LATER

A TV is mounted high on the wall.

                    REPORTER 2
          Back to you, Deb.

EXT. PATIO — MOMENTS LATER

The report is playing on a laptop sitting on a brick wall.

53.

                    REPORTER 5
                Back to you, Sally.

AUDIO STATIC, TV COLOUR BARS SPAGHETTI AND
DISAPPEAR

INTRO ANIMATION

A slick graphic blends images and geometric
shapes, then wraps around to reveal the
title: *Pressure Point*.

AUDIO STATIC, TV COLOUR BARS SPAGHETTI AND
DISAPPEAR

INT. PRESSURE POINT STUDIO — DAY

The host, Francis von Zoofendorfen, looks
into camera.

                    VON ZOOFENDORFEN
                Hello. And welcome to *Pressure
                Point*. I'm your host, Francis
                von Zoofendorfen. Joining me
                today is Mr. Stallward. Mr.
                Stallward is the . . .

ON STALLWARD

                    VON ZOOFENDORFEN
          . . . Provincial Minister
          of Mines and Resources. Mr.
          Stallward, thank you for
          joining us.

INTERCUT — between the two men.

                    STALLWARD
          Thank you for having me. Very
          glad to be here.

                    VON ZOOFENDORFEN
          I am a bit surprised and
          grateful that you were able
          to make it in today since I
          imagine it has been a very busy
          time for your ministry given
          the collapse of that tailings
          pond in the Interior?

                    STALLWARD
          Yes.

                    VON ZOOFENDORFEN
          Yes, yes, absolutely. I
          have to ask you, how is the
          investigation going?

                    STALLWARD
          Ok, well, I think the most
          important thing that we need to
          understand is that no one was
          killed. So that is great news.

ON VON ZOOFENDORFEN

                    VON ZOOFENDORFEN
          That is great news indeed.

                    STALLWARD
          You know, and as far as I
          know . . .

BACK TO STALLWARD

                    STALLWARD
          . . . no one was injured either.

                    VON ZOOFENDORFEN
          No people.

                    STALLWARD
          No humans were hurt. No.

                    VON ZOOFENDORFEN
          Well, yes, that is also good
          news.

                    STALLWARD
          Yes.

                    VON ZOOFENDORFEN
Ah, but here's the one thing
that I would like to ask you
about, even though no people
were injured, which is always
fantastic. I have to ask
you, what about the tens of
thousands of trees that were
wiped out? And, ah, no one has
even estimated, as far as I
know, how many living creatures
were killed.

                    STALLWARD
Yeah. That was terrible. But,
ah, nothing of significant
commercial value was destroyed.

                    VON ZOOFENDORFEN
Commercial value?

                    STALLWARD
Yes. Nothing of use to humans,
so that's great news.

                    VON ZOOFENDORFEN
Oh, ok. And are you sure about
that?

                    STALLWARD
Yes, I'm 100% sure, 63.8%
of the time, according to my
staff.

                    VON ZOOFENDORFEN
Oh, ok. I'm glad you're
batting an average grade on
that point. Um, have you found
out, at least, what caused the
disaster?

                    STALLWARD
Well, um, on a percentage
basis, we don't like to refer
to this as a disaster. That
just blows the whole thing
out of proportion. For our
purposes, I mean, for clarity,
we prefer to refer to it as an
incident.

                    VON ZOOFENDORFEN
An incident? Ok, well, listen,
I'm not one for hyperbole
myself, but we all saw the
pictures, and I have to tell
you that in my opinion, it
was more than an incident. An
entire valley and watershed
were completely wiped out.

                    STALLWARD
Ah, you say wiped out, I say
cleaned out. Disaster just has
such a negative connotation,
that's all I'm saying.

VON ZOOFENDORFEN
In the report that just landed on my desk this morning, doing the comparables to other incidents as you call them, this was one of the world's biggest mining accidents in history. Some say it's in the top five. From most people's perspective, I think it's safe to say it was a disaster.

STALLWARD
I just hate to wallow in super-negatives.

VON ZOOFENDORFEN
Yeah, well, we wouldn't want to do that.

STALLWARD
I mean, a disaster is when you have to call in the army . . . And we sure wouldn't call in the army to watch water flow down a little creek.

VON ZOOFENDORFEN
Ok, well, did you contemplate bringing in the army?

STALLWARD
No. We don't actually have an army.

VON ZOOFENDORFEN
Ok, so let me get this straight. So, even if you had wanted to, you had no ability to call in the army.

STALLWARD
Yes. Zero percent.

VON ZOOFENDORFEN
So, ok, all right then. How about this? What are you doing about the situation, ur, incident, as you call it?

STALLWARD
Well, like I said before, that creek needed a bit of a clean-out.

VON ZOOFENDORFEN
Clean-out? And how do you know that?

STALLWARD
It was in the press release from the company.

VON ZOOFENDORFEN
The mining company that caused the disaster?

STALLWARD
Incident.

VON ZOOFENDORFEN
Incident.

STALLWARD
Yes. Well, practically speaking, and we have to be practical in a situation like this, this incident was really a stroke of luck.

VON ZOOFENDORFEN
A stroke of luck? How so?

STALLWARD
The damage, if you want to call it that, was to nothing but a bunch of rotting logs and some low-grade trees.

VON ZOOFENDORFEN
And how do you know they were low-grade trees?

STALLWARD

Oh, ah, the great people at the mine. In consultation with the friendly folks at ABC Lumber products, who also weighed in with their opinion. Ur, expert opinion. So this whole incident will be judged completely differently in time. It really will be beneficial in the long run. You know, we will end up with a whole pile of new trees.

VON ZOOFENDORFEN

New trees. Right. But what was destroyed was considered valuable habitat? Mature diverse habitat?

STALLWARD

No, no, not at all. Rotting logs are just rotting logs. No value there. Those trees had no commercial value to humans at all. We couldn't use them if we wanted to.

VON ZOOFENDORFEN

Ok, um, how about this then? So what about all the toxic heavy metals?

STALLWARD
What toxic metals? There were none.

VON ZOOFENDORFEN
That's not the evidence I have.

STALLWARD
Well, first of all, there's no such thing as a toxic metal. Either you have metal or you have not metal. Toxic has nothing to do with this. That's just a made-up social media buzzword. Fake news.

Von Zoofendorfen chuckles.

VON ZOOFENDORFEN
Fake news.

STALLWARD
That's the whole point of a mining exercise. The metal, also known as ore I might add, has already been taken out of the rocks and sold. No need to store it on-site. You can't make money storing it in a tailings pond. That would be ridiculous.

VON ZOOFENDORFEN
It certainly would. Let me switch this up. What about the metal sulphides? You know, the acidic leachates that come from the oxidation of the exposed metal?

STALLWARD
Nope. None.

VON ZOOFENDORFEN
Isn't that what the settling pond was for?

STALLWARD
Ah, well, my understanding is, it was for mud.

VON ZOOFENDORFEN
Mud?

STALLWARD
Yep, harmless mud. You see, mud is kind of ugly and they just wanted it contained so it doesn't run all over the place. They just direct it into the pond and—

VON ZOOFENDORFEN
—Hmm—

ON STALLWARD — he brushes his hands against each other.

> STALLWARD
> —it sinks to the bottom so no one can see it. Clean mud.

INTERCUT

> VON ZOOFENDORFEN
> Clean mud.

> STALLWARD
> Clean mud.

> VON ZOOFENDORFEN
> Clean mud.

> STALLWARD
> Clean mud.

BACK TO VON ZOOFENDORFEN

> VON ZOOFENDORFEN
> Ok, got it. Clean mud. So it was just harmless mud that washed down the creek when the dam burst.

> STALLWARD
> Right.

                        VON ZOOFENDORFEN
           Ok, then, what about the fish
           in the creek?

                        STALLWARD
           Not an issue.

                        VON ZOOFENDORFEN
           Really?

                        STALLWARD
           Yes. Think about it. It's just
           common sense. Fish swim, and
           they swim fast. They swam
           with it, or ahead of it. Yeah,
           that's what they do.

                        VON ZOOFENDORFEN
           They swam. The fish just swam
           with it.

                        STALLWARD
           Yep.

BACK TO VON ZOOFENDORFEN

                        VON ZOOFENDORFEN
           How do you know that?

                        STALLWARD
           Because we didn't find any dead
           ones.

VON ZOOFENDORFEN
Oh, so you looked?

STALLWARD
Noooo. . . . Nope.

VON ZOOFENDORFEN
No?

STALLWARD
No. I didn't look. The scientists at the mine, they looked.

VON ZOOFENDORFEN
So they didn't find any dead fish whatsoever?

STALLWARD
Nope.

VON ZOOFENDORFEN
None.

STALLWARD
None.

VON ZOOFENDORFEN
Did any of your staff look?

STALLWARD
Nope. N-nope.

VON ZOOFENDORFEN
Why not?

STALLWARD
Budget cuts.

VON ZOOFENDORFEN
Budget cuts?

STALLWARD
Precisely.

VON ZOOFENDORFEN
So even in an emergency you don't do field surveys?

STALLWARD
But it should also be pointed out, it's not really necessary any more. Everything can be done online now. . . . So, within a few days we got an actual verbal final report on this by voice text, that from a fisheries point of view, there were too many fish in that creek, so the overall harm to the ecosystem was negligible.

VON ZOOFENDORFEN
(indignant)
Negligible! Too many fish! Really?

STALLWARD
I know, can you believe it?

VON ZOOFENDORFEN
Barely.

STALLWARD
There were so many of them. They were all just shrimpy little things. Way too much competition for food, so they were small and undernourished.

VON ZOOFENDORFEN
Ok.

STALLWARD
Yes. So the extra water just kinda pushed them down the creek into the lake. The incident fixed a problem without using a penny of taxpayer dollars.

VON ZOOFENDORFEN
And is there any hard data to back this up? Like an environmental assessment before the mine was built that can back up this rather nebulous "too many fish" claim, perhaps?

STALLWARD
No. But it's a convenient, ur, I mean, great, theory, supported by stellar field work after the fact.

VON ZOOFENDORFEN
All right. I doubt the public thinks it's a great theory. By the way, where'd this theory come from?

STALLWARD
The scientists at the mine came up with it. You know, from all their years of experience?

VON ZOOFENDORFEN
Of wiping out watersheds?

STALLWARD
"Cleaning out" is the professional term.

VON ZOOFENDORFEN
Wow!

STALLWARD
I know. Wow! Putting practical experience to work! I think they call it adaptive management.

Von Zoofendorfen rolls his eyes.

> VON ZOOFENDORFEN
> I might have to adapt my career after this.

Stallward ignores the comment.

> STALLWARD
> Now, the great news is the remaining fish will have more room to move. There will be more bugs per fish to munch on. So, it's really a good thing that happened here, and we can all now witness the rebirthing of an entire ecosystem.

Stallward gives the thumbs-up sign.

> VON ZOOFENDORFEN
> Crazy stuff! So I assume at some point you will release the results of the investigation?

> STALLWARD
> I will have to check with the mining company on that.

> VON ZOOFENDORFEN
> The mining company?

STALLWARD
Yes. I have to check with them to see if we are doing an investigation.

VON ZOOFENDORFEN
So, the mining company is investigating themselves?

STALLWARD
It's actually quite brilliant really, if I say so myself. The new regulations stipulate that they have to investigate themselves and get back to us with their findings. Once upon a time, the Government would have had a bunch of their own scientists do the work. Now, they do the work and it's zero cost to the taxpayer.

Stallward makes a flicking motion with his hand.

STALLWARD
It's a line item I've been able to strike right off the public books. I'm quite proud of it, really.

                    VON ZOOFENDORFEN
               And there is no bias in that?

                    STALLWARD
               Nope. It's properly regulated.
               They wouldn't risk a fine for
               improper reporting.

                    VON ZOOFENDORFEN
               How much is the fine?

                    STALLWARD
               $500.00.

                    VON ZOOFENDORFEN
               $500.00? That's the minimum?

                    STALLWARD
               Hmm. Nooo. I think that's the
               max fine. Yip.

Stallward makes a swish motion with his index
finger.

                    VON ZOOFENDORFEN
               All-righty, then.

Then he pulls his finger across.

                    STALLWARD
               And zip!!

                    VON ZOOFENDORFEN
Ok, then. How about this
little line item? Is the mining
company going to cover the cost
of, ah, the clean-up?

                    STALLWARD
What clean-up?

                    VON ZOOFENDORFEN
The cleaned-out creek and
valley, as you call it?

                    STALLWARD
Nope. Oh no. It's not on their
property. It's public property.
That's part of the Crown's
inventory of useless things.

                    VON ZOOFENDORFEN
Useless things. The tailings
pond and dam are part of the
Crown's inventory of useless
things?

                    STALLWARD
Exactly. All of it is on
public property, so, we, the
Government, the public people,
is responsible.

VON ZOOFENDORFEN
But it's their tailings pond.

STALLWARD
No. You can't expect them to pay for our faulty mud. That would be ludicrous. Wooh. Wooh. That wouldn't be fair. No.

VON ZOOFENDORFEN
Our faulty mud?

STALLWARD
Ah, yeah, the tailings pond was made with our faulty mud, so, therefore our responsibility.

VON ZOOFENDORFEN
Our dirt, that was stacked up a mile high by them and made to be unstable, is our fault?

STALLWARD
Not according to their engineers and their insurance companies, that would pay if it was the mining company's fault. They all say faulty mud.

VON ZOOFENDORFEN
How is that legal?

STALLWARD
It's not a question of
legalities, it's about the
taxpayer taking responsibility
for our own faulty public mud.

VON ZOOFENDORFEN
Even if an incident is caused
by a faulty tailings pond dam
built by a private company with
faulty engineering?

STALLWARD
Well, there is no case to prove
any of that.

Von Zoofendorfen looks skyward.

STALLWARD
Besides, there's an old law.
It's got nothing to do with our
current administration, by the
way. But you have to, by law,
accept water from upstream. So,
we had a duty to accept that
water and not force the mining
company to hold onto it. So the
Government was breaking its own
law.

                    VON ZOOFENDORFEN
          Ok, I'm not a lawyer, but I
          don't think the law refers to a
          dam breaking.

Von Zoofendorfen runs his fingers through his
hair, exasperated.

                    STALLWARD
          The law is the law. We believe
          in the Rule of Law.

                    VON ZOOFENDORFEN
          Wow. Is there an estimate on
          the cost of clean-up?

                    STALLWARD
          About $150 million.

                    VON ZOOFENDORFEN
          One hundred and fifty million
          shamolas! And no fines or
          anything?

                    STALLWARD
          Nope. No. No. NO.

                    VON ZOOFENDORFEN
          Nice. Has the company offered
          any money for the clean-up?

STALLWARD
Nope. No. No. No. Nope.

VON ZOOFENDORFEN
Ok, well, so, who cleans up the lake?

STALLWARD
Well, I've already put forth a proposal with our Cabinet, that we, the taxpayer pay for that, on their behalf.

VON ZOOFENDORFEN
We?

STALLWARD
Yes.

VON ZOOFENDORFEN
Us?

STALLWARD
Yep.

VON ZOOFENDORFEN
The royal us?

STALLWARD
Yep.

                    VON ZOOFENDORFEN
The royally hooped us. The
taxpayers. We're, we are going
to pay for it . . . How in all
of Heaven is that fair?

                    STALLWARD
Well, actually, the company is
eligible for disaster relief.

                    VON ZOOFENDORFEN
Oh my lord, I thought you said
this was an incident?

                    STALLWARD
Environmentally, yes. But from
the mining company's point
of view, it's a financial
disaster. Imagine. Their whole
mine is shut down. So since
the mine is on public property,
it's only fair the taxpayer
assist with the damage to
company property.

                    VON ZOOFENDORFEN
Seriously?

                    STALLWARD
Yes, absolutely.

VON ZOOFENDORFEN
Ok.
  (sucks in a breath)
So. Here's the thing—

STALLWARD
—So I proposed the company receive disaster relief.

VON ZOOFENDORFEN
But I read in your ministry's press release, you say the company will be responsible for the clean-up on their property.

STALLWARD
Oh, they, they should be responsible for cleaning up their own property.

VON ZOOFENDORFEN
Thank you!

STALLWARD
Their office in downtown Vancouver . . . The taxpayer is not paying for their office cleaning staff. No, the public pays for the damage on Crown land, but they have to pay for
(MORE)

                    STALLWARD (CONT'D)
          the cleaning staff at their
          corporate head office. I'm firm
          on that.

                    VON ZOOFENDORFEN
          Wow. Ok, I'm just curious.
          Has this company contributed
          any money to your election
          or to your party in any way
          whatsoever?

                    STALLWARD
          A little bit.

                    VON ZOOFENDORFEN
          A little?

                    STALLWARD
          Ok, a lot.

                    VON ZOOFENDORFEN
          And this has had no bearing on
          how this whole thing has been
          handled?

Von Zoofendorfen looks off-camera at the film crew, presumably for a statistic or something he can use.

                    STALLWARD
          None at all.

VON ZOOFENDORFEN
You're sure?

STALLWARD
Positive.

VON ZOOFENDORFEN
How positive?

STALLWARD
At least twice as positive as I was at 63.8%.

VON ZOOFENDORFEN
So, basically what you are saying is, the company gets the gold and the public gets the shaft.

STALLWARD
Oh, technically, we don't get the shaft. They get to keep that too since they built it.

VON ZOOFENDORFEN
Ok, well, thank you for your time. And for giving us the chance to clear up a muddy situation.

ON STALLWARD

STALLWARD
Oh. You're welcome!

Von Zoofendorfen turns and looks into camera.

VON ZOOFENDORFEN
Well, thanks again for tuning into our show. I've been your host, Francis von Zoofendorfen. This is—

STALLWARD
—Thank you.

VON ZOOFENDORFEN
Whoop. No talking.

ON STALLWARD — he snickers.

VON ZOOFENDORFEN (O.S.)
And that's our show.

BACK TO VON ZOOFENDORFEN

VON ZOOFENDORFEN
I'm Francis von Zoofendorfen, and you've been watching *Pressure Point*.

ON STALLWARD

He smiles into camera and mouths the words "thank you."

                                        FADE TO:

EXT. VANCOUVER SKY (DRONE) — NIGHT

Fireworks explode into the night sky and we . . .

                                        FADE OUT

EPISODE 3:

The Great Escape

K.C. Novak plays Janet Klarrke, the Minister of Environment,
aka the Minister of Unconstitutional Kink-Shaming.

                    ANNOUNCER
          Warning. Hyper-sensitive,
          serious and easily offended
          viewers and politicians may
          find that some dialogue will
          make them laugh. Consult your
          physician before consuming this
          content.

AUDIO STATIC, TV COLOUR BARS SPAGHETTI AND
DISAPPEAR

EXT. VANCOUVER CITY (AERIAL) — NIGHT

A brilliant shot of the downtown core all
lit up.

                    VON ZOOFENDORFEN
          It's time for *Pressure Point*.
          Here's what people have been
          watching and hearing in the
          news this week.

AUDIO STATIC, TV COLOUR BARS SPAGHETTI AND
DISAPPEAR

INT. HOME OFFICE — DAY

ON A COMPUTER MONITOR

87.

EXT. MARINA — DAY

Commercial fishing vessels are tied up to the wharves in Steveston, BC. It's part of a news report.

                  REPORTER 1
        Arguments erupted in court
        today over First Nations
        fishing rights.

EXT. COURTHOUSE — DAY

The reporter is speaking outside the courthouse.

                  REPORTER 1
        According to attendees, there
        was a lot of consultation among
        the parties about whether First
        Nations had been consulted
        enough.

INT. MODERN BAR — CONTINUOUS

The reporter is now on two screens.

                  REPORTER 1
        One thing that was abundantly
        clear was that more consultation
        would be needed for several
                  (MORE)

                    REPORTER 1 (CONT'D)
               hundred more years. Or until
               all fish go extinct, whichever
               comes first.

AUDIO STATIC, TV COLOUR BARS SPAGHETTI AND
DISAPPEAR

INT. BEDROOM - DAY

A TV is perched on top of a dresser. The news
report shows a number of small nets with
white plastic tubing attached to them hanging
over a wharf railing to dry in the sun.

                         REPORTER 2
                    The Squamish Streamkeepers
                    celebrated the 10th anniversary
                    today . . .

The image changes to a close-up of a net full
of herring eggs.

                         REPORTER 2
                    . . . of their herring
                    enhancement projects in Howe
                    Sound and False Creek.

INT. PIZZA PARLOUR - DAY

Two screens are jammed high against the
ceiling. The screen on the right shows
herring being caught by a gillnetter.

                    REPORTER 3
               In a related matter, the
               Department of Fisheries and
               Oceans and Howe Sound Fishing
               Company . . .

ANOTHER SHOT — of the gillnetting as herring
land all over the deck of the boat.

                    REPORTER 3
               . . . celebrated the opening
               of a herring fishery in Howe
               Sound.

INT. BEDROOM — DAY

An iPad sits on a bedside table. A close-up
of a salmon mort tote shows a disgusting pile
of rotting dead fish.

                    REPORTER 4
               Another crop of fish has died
               at a west coast fish farm. The
               pew-trifying slop is enough
               to put anyone off ever eating
               fish again. It's vile and
               disgusting.

INT. HOUSE — DAY

A small radio sits on a window ledge.

                    REPORTER 3
          Officials say it's a great day
          for producing fish farm food in
          British Columbia.

AUDIO STATIC, TV COLOUR BARS SPAGHETTI AND DISAPPEAR

INT. AUTO PARTS SUPPLY STORE — DAY

A television is showing footage of a violent storm.

                    REPORTER 5
          Gale force winds pounded . . .

A reporter is now standing on shore with a calm ocean behind him.

                    REPORTER 5
          . . . the west coast on
          Saturday night,

INT. APARTMENT — CONTINUOUS

A monitor is sitting on a table.

                    REPORTER 5
          . . . leaving residents without
          power and damage to businesses
          up and down the Salish Sea.

INT. PUB — CONTINUOUS

The reporter now appears on two screens side-by-side.

				REPORTER 5
		The Minister of Environment and
		Weather . . .

The screens revert to the stormy ocean.

				REPORTER 5
		. . . stated today that it's
		nothing but a lot of hot
		air . . .

BACK TO REPORTER

				REPORTER 5
		. . . about wind.

INT. CAR — DAY

The radio is on.

				REPORTER 2
		The number of violent storms
		continues to escalate . . .

INT. MODERN PUB — DAY

A TV is showing a violent west coast storm.

                    REPORTER 2
          . . . year after year, as
          global temperatures continue to
          rise.

INT. BUSINESS STORE ROOM — DAY

A TV is sitting on top of a filing cabinet.
The news is on.

                    REPORTER 1
          Over to you!

AUDIO STATIC, TV COLOUR BARS SPAGHETTI AND
DISAPPEAR

INTRO ANIMATION

A slick graphic blends images and geometric
shapes, then wraps around to reveal the
title: *Pressure Point*.

AUDIO STATIC, TV COLOUR BARS SPAGHETTI AND
DISAPPEAR

INT. PRESSURE POINT STUDIO — DAY

The host, Francis von Zoofendorfen, looks
into camera.

                    VON ZOOFENDORFEN
          Hello and welcome to *Pressure
          Point*. I'm your host, Francis
          von Zoofendorfen. And joining
          me today is none other than the
          Minister for the Environment,
          Janet Klarkke.

ON KLARKKE — she is excited and her puckered
lips are making her look like a fish.

WIDER — two shot. Then intercut between them.

                    VON ZOOFENDORFEN
          Minister for the Entire
          Environment. Good for you,
          Madam Klarkke. It is a pleasure
          to have you in the studio.

                    KLARKKE
          It's a pleasure to be here.

                    VON ZOOFENDORFEN
          Wonderful. Excellent. Now,
          let's just get right down to
          it. Quite the storm we had,
          wasn't it?

                    KLARKKE
          Yes. Yes. Worst of the season.

                    VON ZOOFENDORFEN
          Well, one of the things I
          wanted to discuss with you was
          the damage that occurred in the
          fish farm industry. Apparently
          a bunch of open net pens were
          destroyed.

                    KLARKKE
          Yes. Very tragic for those
          pens. Shame on them for being
          open right in the middle of a
          storm. They really should have
          closed the shutters at least.

                    VON ZOOFENDORFEN
          Right.

VON ZOOFENDORFEN — isn't sure if she was
making a joke.

                    VON ZOOFENDORFEN
          Now, tell me. What happened to
          the fish in the pens?

                    KLARKKE
          There were no fish in those
          pens.

                    VON ZOOFENDORFEN
          Well, ok, that is what was
          reported. Yes.

                    KLARKKE
          Precisely.

                    VON ZOOFENDORFEN
          But, what the public wants to
          know, how many fish were in the
          pens before the storm destroyed
          them?

                    KLARKKE
          None, as far as I know.

                    VON ZOOFENDORFEN
          Really?

                    KLARKKE
          Well, when we got to the pens,
          there were no fish. Therefore,
          they must've been empty before
          the storms destroyed them.

                    VON ZOOFENDORFEN (O.S.)
          That's your official answer?

ON VON ZOOFENDORFEN

                    VON ZOOFENDORFEN
          Because our people say one of
          the fish farmers has claimed
          that 350,000 fish escaped.

KLARKKE
That's an erogenous report.

VON ZOOFENDORFEN
I think you mean erroneous.

KLARKKE
Erogenous . . . as opposed to erotic.

VON ZOOFENDORFEN
Oh, ok . . . So, what you're saying is that it was all blown out of proportion?—

KLARKKE
—No . . . no . . . no . . . no sabotage, just, just a little wind.

VON ZOOFENDORFEN
Oh, ok, whatever . . . So, the erogenous report came from the company whose pens were destroyed.

KLARKKE
Yeah, that's fake news.

VON ZOOFENDORFEN
Really?

KLARKKE
That gave me a chill to say that finally. Fake news. They may have had 350,000 fish, but not in those pens. Who knows where people keep fish these days. Maybe in their pens? Maybe in their hats?

VON ZOOFENDORFEN
I would keep my fish where most people keep their fish, in a—

KLARKKE
—See! You don't have an answer. Who knows where they were keeping the fish? All we know for certain is that when our people arrived on-site, there were no fish in those pens.

VON ZOOFENDORFEN
Right, because the fish swam away through the holes in the torn net, which are much bigger than the normally tiny holes. It's all about hole size.

KLARKKE
Stop focusing on holes. These are very domesticated animals and they wouldn't leave their domiciles.

VON ZOOFENDORFEN
We're talking about fish, right?

KLARKKE
Yes. Precisely. Much more intelligent than we give them credit for.

VON ZOOFENDORFEN
Right.

KLARKKE
You can get them to sit and stay. I swear I've seen it.

VON ZOOFENDORFEN
Sure. I mean, yes. If you lay a live fish on a counter, eventually it will stay put. So, yes, a fish out of water will lay and stay to be precise.

KLARKKE
Exactly.

They both laugh.

                    KLARKKE
          We also know that no fish
          escaped because the company
          hasn't put in a claim.

                    VON ZOOFENDORFEN
          Well, ok . . . Well, our
          information is that they did
          put in a claim, a disaster
          relief claim for 350,000 fish.

                    KLARKKE
          Well, yes, but those were for
          different fish. Those are for
          the fish that were just dead.

                    VON ZOOFENDORFEN
          Dead?

                    KLARKKE
          Yes, the company hasn't put in
          a claim for escaped fish, just
          the dead fish. So, they have
          to be dead and we need to see
          dead fish before they can get
          the dead money. Dead money, for
          dead fish, that's how it works.

VON ZOOFENDORFEN
I see. Why don't they just sell the dead fish like they're supposed to?

KLARKKE
Slow down.

VON ZOOFENDORFEN
I will.

KLARKKE
Well, for one thing, if they sold the dead fish they wouldn't be allowed to apply for compensation. And dead fish stink. Who wants that?

VON ZOOFENDORFEN
Not me, that's for sure. So what was wrong with the dead fish?

KLARKKE
This is a news program, correct?

VON ZOOFENDORFEN
Well, at times.

KLARKKE
Well, they couldn't sell them because the fish, besides being dead, were not of good quality.

VON ZOOFENDORFEN
Did they die from disease?

KLARKKE
No, they just died.

VON ZOOFENDORFEN
Just like that? Died for no reason. Did they die of a tumour? Heart disease? Stroke, perhaps? Smoking too much?

KLARKKE
Fish don't smoke. The water makes it hard to light cigarettes, silly.

VON ZOOFENDORFEN
Well, they sell smoked salmon in the stores. It had to come from somewhere.

KLARKKE
Good point. Well, remember how your grandparents just one day up and died?

VON ZOOFENDORFEN
Ok, yes.

KLARKKE
Just like that.

VON ZOOFENDORFEN
All at once? The whole population just died like they had all taken suicide pills. That can happen?

KLARKKE
Yes. Have you ever heard of mass die-offs?

VON ZOOFENDORFEN
What, is that like sympathy deaths? They see one die and they decide to join them?

KLARRKE
Something like that.

VON ZOOFENDORFEN
Ok.

KLARKKE
Then they all sink.

VON ZOOFENDORFEN
Really? Fish can sink?

                    KLARKKE
Yes.

                    VON ZOOFENDORFEN
Sink or swim. Ah! Is that where
the term comes from?

                    KLARKKE
Yeesss.

WIDER

                    VON ZOOFENDORFEN
Oh my goodness. Oh, you know
what? This *is* a news program,
because I am learning so many
new things about fish. Oh my
goodness gracious. Now, here's
the thing.

ON VON ZOOFENDORFEN — as he glances at his
notes.

                    VON ZOOFENDORFEN
I'm told fish escaping from
these nets is rather common in
spite of damage by storms?

                    KLARKKE
Well, my predecessor followed
this quite closely, and he said
they lost one or two fish.

VON ZOOFENDORFEN
Like per farm, per week . . .
or what do you mean?

KLARKKE
No. For the whole coast. All
time.

VON ZOOFENDORFEN
All time. Wow! That stat sounds
unreal. So that makes you
unreal!

KLARKKE
No, I'm for real.
    (giggles)

VON ZOOFENDORFEN
Wow! I would say this must be
some kind of an international
fish farm record.

KLARKKE
I know, right! And only in
Canada!

VON ZOOFENDORFEN
Wow, that is, speaking about
only in Canada . . . Here's
something I found to be a
little bit curious. According
    (MORE)

                    VON ZOOFENDORFEN (CONT'D)
          to my notes here, "sport
          fishermen have been catching
          Atlantic salmon in our Pacific
          west coast streams" for some
          years now. What do you say
          to the folks who have seen
          or caught Atlantic salmon in
          Pacific Coast streams?

Von Zoofendorfen waves vaguely toward the
east coast. Klarkke nods.

                    KLARKKE
          Well, it's obvious. Those are
          wild fish.

                    VON ZOOFENDORFEN
          Not farmed fish?

                    KLARKKE
          Not farmed fish.

                    VON ZOOFENDORFEN
          You're sure about that?

                    KLARKKE
          Absolutely sure.

                    VON ZOOFENDORFEN
          Ok, so, Atlantic salmon on the
          Pacific coast are wild?

KLARKKE
Yes.

VON ZOOFENDORFEN
So, let's be clear about this. Fish that are normally found off the east coast of Canada, say, off the shores of New Brunswick in the Atlantic Ocean, are also wild fish on this coast?

KLARKKE
Yes.

VON ZOOFENDORFEN
I assume they are called Atlantic salmon for a reason.

KLARKKE
Yes, I think it has to do with the colour of their eyes. They kinda have that Nova Scotian eye colour going for them.

VON ZOOFENDORFEN
That sounds fishy to me.

KLARKKE
Me too! Isn't it wonderful that fish have fishy eyes?

VON ZOOFENDORFEN
Well, let me ask you this. How did they get established on the Pacific coast?

KLARKKE
Well, they bought a ticket and hopped on a plane, of course.
(giggles)
They swam, I would assume.

Von Zoofendorfen laughs.

VON ZOOFENDORFEN
They swam. That I agree with, the fish swam. But my people tell me they actually swam from the local fish farms.

KLARKKE
Well, no . . . My people's information is that they actually swam via the Arctic Ocean. Fish like to wander. We all like to travel, right? Well, fish are no different. They are just simply exploring the great outdoors and on vacation. Who knows? It's hard to read a fish's mind, you know.

VON ZOOFENDORFEN
Really?

KLARKKE
Hmm. Mmmm. They have these amazing poker faces. They should play cards.

VON ZOOFENDORFEN
Wow. Ok. But my people say the fins are all worn like the farm fish in the fish farms pens. This is typical damage from swimming inside net pens.

KLARKKE
That's heresy.

VON ZOOFENDORFEN
You mean hearsay.

KLARKKE
Ok, I'll let you in on a bit of orthodox scientific doctrine. My people say it's just from rubbing up against icebergs, getting scratched up like what happened to the *Titanic*. You know, like getting bumps and bruises swimming in tight icy crevices.

                    VON ZOOFENDORFEN
          Icy crevices. Don't get me
          going on that point. My people
          think that's just a bunch of
          malarkey.

                    KLARKKE
          Well, would you believe it's
          from spawning? Because, ah,
          procreation can be a very rough
          business for these salmon, you
          know. And my people gave me
          that as an alternate excuse,
          scenario that it was from
          spawning.

                    VON ZOOFENDORFEN
          So, are you saying that
          Atlantic salmon travel to the
          Pacific coast to spawn?

                    KLARKKE
          Exactly.

                    VON ZOOFENDORFEN
          With what fish?

                    KLARKKE
          We're investigating, but I hear
          that young Pacific salmon are,
          well, enticing and attractive
                    (MORE)

KLARKKE (CONT'D)
to Atlantic salmon, which makes them swim into the streams.

VON ZOOFENDORFEN
Are you suggesting that there might be something criminal going on here?

KLARKKE
There could be. All of this activity is occurring under the cloak of water, so who knows what's going on down there?

VON ZOOFENDORFEN
Ok, so if we pull all this together, it sounds like you're saying that adult Atlantic salmon are coming to Pacific streams to have sex with our Pacific salmon juveniles?

KLARKKE
Well, we choose to not go into the bedrooms of those good old Canadian fish. It's against the constitution, you know. Besides, they have privacy rights.

VON ZOOFENDORFEN
Fish have privacy rights?

                    KLARKKE
It's a new thing. Our
government believes that all
the rights we humans have
should also apply to other
species, including fish.

                    VON ZOOFENDORFEN
Wow. Ok, so these Atlantics
are effectively foreign sexual
predators and they are swimming
in our Pacific streams to seek
out innocent juvenile fish in
local Pacific waters? And that
is why Atlantic fish are on the
Pacific coast?

                    KLARKKE
Now, wait a minute, I don't
care for you kink-shaming our
Canadian fish!

                    VON ZOOFENDORFEN
What?

                    KLARKKE
I am insulted that you would
imply that Atlantic fish are
foreign sexual predators. They
are all Canadian fish and there
is nothing foreign about them.
So what fish do behind waves
                    (MORE)

                    KLARKKE (CONT'D)
of water is really none of our
business. We have a policy of
staying out of the bedrooms of
our indigenous fish . . . and
they can be predators if they
want.

                    VON ZOOFENDORFEN
Ah, well, geez, ok . . .
Well, if they came from the
Atlantic Ocean . . . that is
a long, long, long way away. I
don't think, and this is just
opinion, but I'm going to
extrapolate it from various
things that I've heard from
you. I'm going to go out on
a limb and say that these
Atlantic salmon are swimming in
foreign waters.

                    KLARKKE
Well, even if that is the case,
salmon are migratory, you know.
And they are great at swimming
and that sort of thing. So a
swimming holiday is not out
of the realm of possibilities.
Swimming is probably the thing
that they do best.

VON ZOOFENDORFEN
Holy mackerel, you got me on that one. You know what? I'm gonna, I will give you that, they are good swimmers. Fish are known for swimming. Wow. Yes.

KLARKKE
And they certainly didn't swim south through the Panama Canal.

VON ZOOFENDORFEN
Was that even considered?

KLARKKE
Well, my people say salmon don't like tropical waters. It's too hot. Or sharks. My people say they don't like sharks.

VON ZOOFENDORFEN
Ok, so you're saying they don't like sharks and that's why they went through the Arctic.

KLARKKE
My people, hypothetically speaking, said it wasn't a good enough excuse, ur, possibility, so we ruled it out.

VON ZOOFENDORFEN
Ok, well, my people consider Atlantic salmon to be an exotic species on the BC coast.

KLARKKE
There you go. First you say they're foreign and now you're saying they're exotic, trying to kink-shame our good old Canadian fish again.

VON ZOOFENDORFEN
That is not—

KLARKKE
—They aren't considered an exotic species in Canadian Atlantic waters, are they?

VON ZOOFENDORFEN
I guess not.

KLARKKE
And in Canada, all Canadians are Canadians under the eyes of the constitution?

VON ZOOFENDORFEN
I've heard rumours to that effect.

KLARKKE
And it's the same for our fish. All Canadian fish are equal in the eyes of the law. Nothing exotic about them. They are all Canadian fish. And I stand strongly on that.

VON ZOOFENDORFEN
Ok, so you're saying that the Government's position is these fish are native no matter where they come from?

KLARKKE
Oh now, well, bringing First Nations claims into the discussion isn't helpful.

VON ZOOFENDORFEN
I beg your pardon? What are you talking about?

KLARKKE
First Nations haven't ever caught Atlantic salmon on the Pacific coast, so any treaty negotiations must not include Atlantic salmon for this coast.

                    VON ZOOFENDORFEN
          Um. Hum. You know that "native"
          or "indigenous" are terms that
          can also apply to fish?

                    KLARKKE
          Exactly. Natively caught fish.
          Indigenously processed fish.

Von Zoofendorfen doesn't know how to even
respond to this, so he ignores it.

                    VON ZOOFENDORFEN
          So, what you are saying is that
          because Atlantic salmon are
          Canadian fish and are native to
          Canada's east coast, that said
          Atlantics are also indigenous
          to the Pacific?

                    KLARKKE
          Well, only when it's
          convenient.

                    VON ZOOFENDORFEN
          Ok.

                    KLARKKE
          They are non-native fish when
          it comes to First Nations
          negotiations.

VON ZOOFENDORFEN
So you're trying to extinguish
First Nations claims when it
comes to Atlantic salmon?

KLARKKE
Extinguish is too harsh.
Extinct them. Extinct seems
less permanent. Oh.

VON ZOOFENDORFEN
That seems like a very naughty
word when it comes to the
survival of a species.

Klarkke flashes a naughty grin.

KLARKKE
It is, isn't it?

Klarkke wags her finger around the room at
the people out of view.

KLARKKE
We all know, in this room, that
only regular non-native people
are the only ones that should
own Atlantic salmon.

VON ZOOFENDORFEN
Which is what might happen if we keep doing what we're doing the way we're doing it.

KLARKKE
Exactly.

VON ZOOFENDORFEN
Yes, ok, well. I'm sure First Nations folks will wholeheartedly agree with your position on this.

KLARKKE
I try to be clear!

VON ZOOFENDORFEN
Well, you know what? I feel that you are crystal clear. As clear as the oceans of the Atlantic or the Pacific. Or the Arctic . . . And there you have it, ladies and gentlemen. According to the Government, Atlantic salmon on the Pacific coast are native fish not subject to First Nations claims. You heard it here first.

KLARKKE
Exactly.

VON ZOOFENDORFEN
Thanks for your time, Minister Klarkke.

KLARKKE
My people say thank you.

VON ZOOFENDORFEN
It's been nice talking to your people.

KLARKKE
And they've liked talking to your people. Except when you were kink-shaming good old Canadian fish.

VON ZOOFENDORFEN
Well, we'll just have to refrain from that in the future, won't we?

They both laugh uncomfortably.

VON ZOOFENDORFEN
Thank you again so much for your time, Madam Klarkke, it has been a delight. It has been a pleasure.

                    KLARKKE
          Ooh.
                    (giggles)

ON KLARKKE

                    VON ZOOFENDORFEN
          Well, there you have it.
          Atlantic salmon on the Pacific
          coast are native wild fish
          not subject to First Nations
          claims. And they are not
          foreign sexual predators
          looking for a quickie with our
          Pacific salmon. Thank you very
          much, Minister Klarkke.

Klarkke puckers her lips like a fish and
we . . .

                                        FADE TO:

EXT. VANCOUVER SKY (DRONE) — NIGHT

Fireworks explode into the night sky and we
go to . . .

                                        FADE OUT

EPISODE 4:

Fishy Oil Slick

Alex Zahara plays Allyn Smyyth, the Official Coast Guard Spokesperson, aka the Official Spokesperson for Oily Manipulations.

                    ANNOUNCER
          Warning. Hyper-sensitive,
          serious and easily offended
          viewers and politicians may
          find that some dialogue will
          make them laugh. Consult your
          physician before consuming this
          content.

AUDIO STATIC, TV COLOUR BARS SPAGHETTI AND
DISAPPEAR

EXT. VANCOUVER CITY (AERIAL) - NIGHT

A brilliant shot of the downtown core all
lit up.

                  VON ZOOFENDORFEN
          It's time for *Pressure Point*.
          Here's what people have been
          watching and hearing in the
          news this week.

AUDIO STATIC, TV COLOUR BARS SPAGHETTI AND
DISAPPEAR

INT. RECREATION ROOM - NIGHT

A TV is on. A shot of oil tankers cuts to a
news reporter.

                    REPORTER 1
          Standing here on Kits beach,
          you would never know that . . .

ON REPORTER 1

                    REPORTER 1
          . . . this was the site of the
          largest oil spill in Burrard
          Inlet in 48 years. No police.
          No coast guard. No emergency
          responders.

INT. BAR — NIGHT

The same news.

                    REPORTER 1
          No oil containment booms.
          Nothing. But in fact, this is
          almost the same response there
          was the last time bunker oil
          was spilled by a freighter, in
          1973.

TV screen above a serving bar.

                    REPORTER 1
          Almost. At least then,
          newspapers reported that "the
          oil spill response has been
                        (MORE)

                    REPORTER 1 (CONT'D)
               haphazard and comical at
               best." So at least there was
               a response. But instead, we're
               waiting here for anything. A
               comical response would be
               welcome.

INT. RESTAURANT — CONTINUOUS

Looking up at the TV high on a wall.

                    REPORTER 1
               It appears our oil responders
               have ghosted us. This has been
               Bradley Duffy with Channel
               Therlve news. Back to you, Al.

AUDIO STATIC, TV COLOUR BARS SPAGHETTI AND
DISAPPEAR

INT. KITCHEN — DAY

A radio is perched on a country craft cabinet
alongside an assortment of plants.

                    REPORTER 2
               Scientists at the Spuzzum
               Science Centre revealed in
               their 2021 report that not all
               oil spills are equal.

INT. SPARSE OFFICE — CONTINUOUS

The report continues on a laptop. An orange oil boom is containing some oil floating on water.

                    REPORTER 2
          Bitumen, for example, sinks,
          while diesel floats.

ANOTHER ANGLE — barely any oil.

                    REPORTER 2
          So, if we are going to have a
          spill, vote for diesel!

INT. HOME OFFICE — DAY

A TV is on a desk.

THE NEWS — shows an emergency worker carrying a bag of oil-contaminated pads in a yellow garbage bag.

MEN — work in a boat organizing oil spill materials.

A BOOM — surrounds the end of a wharf.

                    REPORTER 3
          Here we are again. Two oil
          spills in a single month.

A MAN — tosses some oil-soak pads over the slick below the dock.

A REPORTER — for The Green Channel is wearing a hazard worksite vest over her jacket and standing at the end of the wharf.

> REPORTER 3
> Just a month ago, local residents were first responders at the oil spill that occurred just over there in Burrard Inlet.

ON TANKERS — anchored in Burrard Inlet at sunset.

> REPORTER 3
> Not to be outdone by events in 1973,

ON A STILL — of the 1973 oil spill.

> REPORTER 3
> . . . when two oil spills occurred a month apart.

BACK TO REPORTER 3

                    REPORTER 3
          History has unfortunately
          repeated itself. But at least
          this time the oil response is
          eerily quick and thorough.

AUDIO STATIC, TV COLOUR BARS SPAGHETTI AND
DISAPPEAR

INT. CAR — DAY

                    REPORTER 2
          A government report just
          released to the public states
          that the frequency of oil
          spills has been dropping in
          recent weeks.

ON A RADIO — radio static clears to reveal
the voice of a reporter.

                    REPORTER 3
          By a government press release,

INT. NEW RESTAURANT — CONTINUOUS

A wall-mounted TV is turned on to the Non
Cents News. A reporter is at a beach and we
see the ocean in the background.

                    REPORTER 3
          . . . that claimed oil spills
          are dropping weekly. A federal
          political candidate for the
          next election posted today
          that . . .

INT. HOME OFFICE — CONTINUOUS

ON A COMPUTER MONITOR — tuned into the same
Non Cents News report.

                    REPORTER 3
          . . . "the ultimate goal should
          be to reduce the frequency
          of . . .

The report goes to a bad oil slick.

                    REPORTER 3
          . . . oil spills to just one a
          day. One expert thought that as
          impossible as it sounds, one a
          day should be achievable."

INT. BEDROOM OFFICE — LATER

A tablet is perched on a desk and is
displaying The Green Channel.

                    REPORTER 3
               This is Kathy Wong for The
               Green Channel.

AUDIO STATIC, TV COLOUR BARS SPAGHETTI AND
DISAPPEAR

INTRO ANIMATION

A slick graphic blends images and geometric
shapes, then wraps around to reveal the
title: *Pressure Point*.

AUDIO STATIC, TV COLOUR BARS SPAGHETTI AND
DISAPPEAR

INT. PRESSURE POINT STUDIO — DAY

The host, Francis von Zoofendorfen, looks
into camera.

                    VON ZOOFENDORFEN
               Hello and welcome to *Pressure
               Point*! I'm your host, Francis
               von Zoofendorfen.

Von Zoofendorfen is in his usual spot.

                    VON ZOOFENDORFEN
               And joining me today is Mr.
               Allyn Smyyth, spokesperson for
               the federal coast guard. Mr.
               Smyyth, welcome to the show!

Smyyth puts out his hand as if offering a handshake.

INTERCUT

              SMYYTH
    Thanks for having me, Francis.

            VON ZOOFENDORFEN
    Thank you for being here. Now,
    let's just get right to it,
    shall we?

Smyyth nods.

            VON ZOOFENDORFEN
    You must be very pleased at
    the response to this latest oil
    spill?

              SMYYTH
    Well, I think "pleased" is an
    odd word to use when describing
    an oil spill.

ON SMYYTH

            VON ZOOFENDORFEN
    Well, yes, of course.

                    SMYYTH
I hear you, but generally
speaking I look at oil spills
as quite negative. So, my
reaction to an oil spill is
negative until it gets cleaned
up. Then it's a positive.

                    VON ZOOFENDORFEN
Yes. I mean, the quickness at
how fast your team got to the
spill. I have to say, that was
very impressive.

                    SMYYTH
Yes. We were Johnny-on-the-
spot. Quick is us. Yes.
          (whistles)

                    VON ZOOFENDORFEN
Exactly. And what a
coincidence, I have to say,
that this occurred just 60
days after the last oil spill
in Burrard Inlet where no one
responded at all.

                    SMYYTH
Yes. I thought you might
mention that. That original
spill was a tragic incident.
          (MORE)

SMYYTH (CONT'D)
Our government realized there was a gap and it needed to be addressed. So, we pivoted and fine-tuned the coordination response through the coast guard.

VON ZOOFENDORFEN
Fantastic. But didn't your government create the gap by closing the Burrard coast guard station in the first place?

SMYYTH
Well, that's one way to look at it. Yes.

VON ZOOFENDORFEN
Is there more than one way?

SMYYTH
I'm glad you asked. There are always growing pains to be expected when retooling the very inefficient government that we inherited. And bricks and mortar operations are pretty passé these days.

VON ZOOFENDORFEN
They are, are they?

                    SMYYTH
          Yes. So now the coast guard
          just floats around, deeking
          here, weaving there. Kinda like
          an old-time boxer, floats like
          an oil tanker, stings like a
          torpedo.

                    VON ZOOFENDORFEN
          Stings like a torpedo.

                    SMYYTH
          Yes, yes, floating around
          makes us much more flexible
          and that's good for our
          environmental response times.
          Way, way, way more responsive.
          Yes, so we can blast a problem
          before it blows up.

WIDER — Smyyth snaps his fingers. He's
clearly a cheerleader for the service.

                    VON ZOOFENDORFEN
          So, waaay more flexible. What
          if you are way off in the wrong
          direction, like up north, when
          a spill happens on the south
          coast?

SMYYTH
Our intelligence on the ground, that's what keeps us close to where the oil spills are going to occur. We know where to be.

He smirks.

SMYYTH
So, we put our people right where spills are likely to happen, not where there is a good place for a station.

VON ZOOFENDORFEN
Well, I guess it worked. You got there as quick as a torpedo and the clean-up team was very impressive.

SMYYTH
Oh yes, well, we take oil spills very seriously in Canada. And our government and, may I add, our party especially, takes the shipping of oil very seriously. We want to get the oil out of Canadian waters as fast as possible and the Canadian people can expect nothing but the best from us.

                    VON ZOOFENDORFEN
          I guess that's good. Was there
          any damage to, ah, any of the
          fish or life in the area?

                    SMYYTH
          Oh. No, no, no, no. Absolutely
          not.

                    VON ZOOFENDORFEN
          Oh, and how would you know that
          exactly? I mean, it's only been
          12 hours since the spill.

                    SMYYTH
          Fair question, but there are no
          fish in the area.

                    VON ZOOFENDORFEN
          Really.

                    SMYYTH
          Well, it's in the heart of an
          industrial area. And it's been
          a cesspool for years. All the
          industrial waste and human
          feces in there from all the
          live-a-boards dumping their
          sewage. It's just been a real
          environmental nightmare, you
          see. But this all happened
                         (MORE)

SMYYTH (CONT'D)
long, long, long before our
government ever came into
office.

VON ZOOFENDORFEN
Long before!

SMYYTH
Yes. Long, long, long, LONG
before.

VON ZOOFENDORFEN
Oh, so I, if I have this right,
it was long, long, loooonnngg
before your government was in
office.

SMYYTH
That's right. Not our fault at
all. I want to be clear about
that.

VON ZOOFENDORFEN
Ok, so, just to be clear. Not
your fault.

Von Zoofendorfen looks down at his notes.
Then back up as though he had to confirm what
he just heard from Smyyth.

SMYYTH
Yes, absolutely not our fault.

VON ZOOFENDORFEN
I think we got it. Not your fault.

Smyyth shakes his head.

SMYYTH
Yes. Yes. Not our fault.

VON ZOOFENDORFEN
Good to have cleared up that point.

SMYYTH
Yes, it's important to have accurate records. You know the old saying.

VON ZOOFENDORFEN
What's that?

SMYYTH
If you don't know history, history is likely to repeat itself. I think that's how it goes.

ON VON ZOOFENDORFEN

VON ZOOFENDORFEN
Actually, I think Satayana said, "Those that can't remember the past are condemned to repeat it."

SMYYTH
Precisely. That's it.

VON ZOOFENDORFEN
But in this case, might I suggest that those remembering the past decided to repeat it?

SMYYTH
What?

VON ZOOFENDORFEN
What if I were to say to you that I've got a current ecosystem survey of False Creek? This is the one that was published literally just days, if not hours, perhaps even weeks or minutes ago. And apparently there are a lot of juvenile fish in False Creek in spite of all the development in the area.

SMYYTH
Well, I would say that's due to our, ah, you know, good stewardship of the environment generally.

VON ZOOFENDORFEN
Really, this is amazing. You've only been in power for one year and you have already turned around the ecosystem in False Creek.

SMYYTH
Absolutely, yes, we brought it back to life. It's what happens when you have a good government.

Smyyth pounds his fist into the palm of his other hand.

SMYYTH
We get things done.

VON ZOOFENDORFEN
That is wonderful. So I would guess that this good government would be testing to see if any of your fish have been affected in any way?

SMYYTH
No, not at all.

VON ZOOFENDORFEN
No? Why's that?

SMYYTH
It's not necessary. Well, think about it. The good thing about fish is they can swim and they can swim fast. So, when there are toxins around and they get one whiff of danger, they scram right out of the area. They have pretty awesome flight or fight mechanisms. And in this case they would put the flight mechanism into overdrive, so to speak.

VON ZOOFENDORFEN
Ok, a bit optimistic I would suggest, but what about the invertebrates?

SMYYTH
I don't know much about invert statistics.

VON ZOOFENDORFEN
No, I'm, I'm talking about things like mussels and all that stuff that doesn't actually swim. You know, invertebrates.

SMYYTH
Oh, right, those in-vert-e-BRATS.

Von Zoofendorfen mimics Smyyth.

VON ZOOFENDORFEN
Yes, right, the, the in-vert-e-brats.

SMYYTH
Right.

VON ZOOFENDORFEN
Right, ok.

SMYYTH
Well, we've seen no effect. They must have a good defence mechanism. Turtling, I think they call it. But you know, even if they get hit by this, well, I guess that's what natural selection is all about,
(MORE)

SMYYTH (CONT'D)
isn't it? If you can't move out
of the way of danger, well, you
perish. The circle of life, as
they say.

Smyyth looks like he's about to burst into a
song, but von Zoofendorfen puts up his hand
and interjects.

VON ZOOFENDORFEN
Please. Let's not hurt anyone's
ears.

He drops his hand.

VON ZOOFENDORFEN
I don't think I've heard that
interpretation of natural
selection before.

SMYYTH
Well, that's because we've
a lot of new ideas with this
government. We're forward
thinkers.

VON ZOOFENDORFEN
Or, or some people might say,
some very old ideas.

SMYYTH

Precisely. Old ideas are tried and true and they work over time. And when the old ideas don't work, we put in new ideas right away. It's startling, really, how efficient that is. And of course, we shun new ideas, especially when they are bad ideas.

VON ZOOFENDORFEN

You won't get an argument out of me on that one. You take out the old and put in the new and if it doesn't work—

SMYYTH

—You have a bunch of goo.

VON ZOOFENDORFEN

Right. I believe that is the actual saying.

Smyyth beams.

VON ZOOFENDORFEN

Right. But you have to admit, this is an enormous stroke of luck. You know, considering that all of this came so close

(MORE)

VON ZOOFENDORFEN (CONT'D)
to an election in which the governing party seems to be trailing in the polls. Ah, I mean, I'm sure your response and efficient clean-up is much appreciated in the Prime Minister's office.

SMYYTH
Couldn't have planned it better, um, yes, quite fortunate, um, you know what I mean.

VON ZOOFENDORFEN
You used to work there before this latest post? At the PMO, correct?

Smyyth suddenly gets defensive.

SMYYTH
Yeah, I did.

VON ZOOFENDORFEN
Ah, and you worked on the last federal campaign, didn't you?

SMYYTH
Yes. Yes, I did. I serve at the pleasure of the Prime Minister.

VON ZOOFENDORFEN
And you worked on the last federal campaign? As a strategist?

SMYYTH
Well, yes.

VON ZOOFENDORFEN
So I'm sure the Prime Minister is pleased with your work here?

SMYYTH
Well, that's for the Prime Minister to decide. But we do our best to have our ears to the water or the ground and help where needed.

VON ZOOFENDORFEN
Speaking of having your ear to the ground . . . I received a note that one of the live-a-board residents, as they call them, down in False Creek happened to notice the spill when it was first occurring.

SMYYTH
Not possible.

VON ZOOFENDORFEN
Why is that not possible?

SMYYTH
There was no one there.

VON ZOOFENDORFEN
How do you know there was no one there?

Smyyth gets angry.

SMYYTH
Well, logically there couldn't have been a witness or the spill wouldn't have happened. Someone would've called for help before it became serious. If someone was there, they would've stopped it.

VON ZOOFENDORFEN
Ok, so by your logic, a serious oil spill can only occur when no one is around to witness it.

Smyyth looks sheepish.

SMYYTH
That's right. Serious oil spills only happen when no one is around . . . at least at first.

VON ZOOFENDORFEN
Ok. Well, not one to put a thorn in your definition, real saying, but we have a witness that claims there was someone on board a fishing vessel and they were pumping diesel fuel out of its main tank into the water.

SMYYTH
That's ridiculous. Who would do that? It didn't happen.

VON ZOOFENDORFEN
Ok, well, according to the witness they told the fisherman that they were spilling fuel.

SMYYTH
Again, not possible, didn't happen.

VON ZOOFENDORFEN
Well, how do you explain the
fact that our testing found
that the oil was not oil at all
but, in fact, diesel fuel?

SMYYTH
And where did you get the
testing done?

VON ZOOFENDORFEN
At an independent laboratory.

SMYYTH
Oh, really. I want a name.

VON ZOOFENDORFEN
No. I can't give that to you.

SMYYTH
There are no independent,
reliable laboratories in
Canada. It's not allowed.

VON ZOOFENDORFEN
Well, whatever, and the witness
also said that a coast guard
vessel was tied up to the
vessel that was spilling the
diesel fuel. At 3 o'clock in
the morning.

SMYYTH
Well, our staff heard about the spill in the middle of the night and we got there as fast as possible way before any so-called witnesses that don't know what they are talking about.

VON ZOOFENDORFEN
But your news release says you arrived at 6 o'clock in the A.M.

SMYYTH
That's a typo. We got there hours earlier, like 3:00 A.M.

VON ZOOFENDORFEN
That we can agree on, but it sounds like you're changing your story.

SMYYTH
I am not.

VON ZOOFENDORFEN
Ok, how about this? Apparently one of your staff told the witness to go away.

SMYYTH
Typo. I mean, not possible. We don't have any staff. Just co-conspirators. Um, colleagues helping on the ground.

VON ZOOFENDORFEN
Or ocean, I would say. And we also learned from the staff here that neither vessel normally moors at that wharf. How do you explain the likelihood of that?

Smyyth runs his fingers through his hair. He's in trouble and he knows it.

SMYYTH
I told you I don't do subversive statistics. Besides, we're all floaties. Um, floating around all the time. We don't tie up to wharves.

VON ZOOFENDORFEN
I agree you are a bunch of floaties.

SMYYTH
Floating ships.

VON ZOOFENDORFEN
Sure.

SMYYTH
We're always moving around.

VON ZOOFENDORFEN
Well, you have to admit it's quite the coincidence that two boats, a fishing boat and a coast guard boat, moored together at night, in a place they don't normally go, and one spills diesel and the other one leads the clean-up. I would have to say that's quite the chain of events, wouldn't you say?

SMYYTH
You know what?

VON ZOOFENDORFEN
What?

SMYYTH
This is obviously a rumour started by the opposition. And you've been suckered into this whole pile of nonsense.

                    VON ZOOFENDORFEN
          I guess the real question then
          is, was this spill a deliberate
          spill? A spill to demonstrate
          the Government had fixed
          the non-existent oil spill
          response?

                    SMYYTH
          That's preposterous!

He jabs his finger at von Zoofendorfen's
face.

                    SMYYTH
          That is an outrageous
          accusation. That would be
          vandalism and illegal.

                    VON ZOOFENDORFEN
          It would be. And I suspect
          unethical.

                    SMYYTH
          Exactly.

                    VON ZOOFENDORFEN
          Right.

Smyyth shakes his fist at von Zoofendorfen.

SMYYTH
We would never stoop to such a low-brow trick. I think there should be an investigation.

VON ZOOFENDORFEN
My thinking exactly.

SMYYTH
I'm going to—

VON ZOOFENDORFEN
—Sink like an oil ship and sting like diesel fuel in the eyes, perhaps?

SMYYTH
The Prime Minister is not going to be happy about this.

VON ZOOFENDORFEN
I wouldn't be surprised by that!

BACK TO SMYYTH

SMYYTH
Good. We finally agree on something! Wonderful!

VON ZOOFENDORFEN
Yes.

SMYYTH
You, you know what I'm going to do?

VON ZOOFENDORFEN
What?

SMYYTH
I'm going to ah, um, well it . . .

Smyyth stands up. He reaches over and grabs von Zoofendorfen's tie and rips it out of his vest.

SMYYTH
Your little tie sucks. I'm out of here.

Von Zoofendorfen sits back in his chair with a smirk, then looks into camera.

VON ZOOFENDORFEN
Thank you, once again, for tuning in. Until next time, I'm your host, Francis von Zoofendorfen, and this has been *Pressure Point!*

Smyyth, from somewhere off the set.

SMYYTH (O.S.)
How do I get out of here?
Where's the door?

VON ZOOFENDORFEN
It's back to the left! Someone
help this, this—

Suddenly Smyyth walks across the set.

SMYYTH
—Jackass.

VON ZOOFENDORFEN
You took the words right out of
my mouth. Please help him find
the door.

SMYYTH
Jerk!!

VON ZOOFENDORFEN
Someone! He's exiting into the
alley.

A door slams.

VON ZOOFENDORFEN
Now he's locked himself in
the washroom. I think he's
relieving himself.

                    SMYYTH
                  (muffled)
          No comment.

Von Zoofendorfen looks back into camera.

                    VON ZOOFENDORFEN
          Well, that's another exciting
          conclusion to our show. I am
          Francis von Zoofendorfen and
          this has been *Pressure Point*.

                                        FADE TO:

EXT. VANCOUVER SKY (DRONE) — NIGHT

Fireworks explode into the night sky and
we . . .

                                        FADE OUT

EPISODE 5:

Nothing but Pipeline Dreams

Zak Santiago plays Roberto Gonzelezz, the Energy Minister, aka the Minister of Questionable Transparency.

                    ANNOUNCER
          Warning. The following program
          contains rude, sassy, adult-
          themed, comical material.
          Hyper-sensitive, serious and
          easily offended viewers and
          politicians may find that some
          dialogue will make them laugh.
          Consult your physician before
          consuming this content.

AUDIO STATIC, TV COLOUR BARS SPAGHETTI AND DISAPPEAR

EXT. VANCOUVER CITY (AERIAL) — NIGHT

A brilliant shot of the downtown core all lit up.

                    VON ZOOFENDORFEN
          It's time for *Pressure Point*.
          Here's what people have been
          watching and hearing in the
          news this week.

AUDIO STATIC, TV COLOUR BARS SPAGHETTI AND DISAPPEAR

INT. HOME SHOP — DAY

The TV is on, with a news report underway. An aerial view of the tar sands is on screen.

                    REPORTER 1
               Protesters took to the streets
               today . . .

EXT. DECK — CONTINUOUS

A radio sits on a stand overlooking a
residential neighbourhood.

                    REPORTER 1
               . . . and then to pipeline
               easements to voice their
               objections to the shipping and
               use of fossil fuels.

INT. BEDROOM — DAY

A small TV is turned on to a climate protest.
Protesters are marching downtown. A gravelly
voice is speaking . . .

                    REPORTER 2
               Climate change protests have
               spread . . .

INT. WORKSHOP — CONTINUOUS

A radio is blaring out the report.

                    REPORTER 2
               . . . across the globe today in
               a worldwide effort to stop the
               use of fossil fuels.

EXT. BACKYARD — DAY

A small transistor radio sits on a rock wall in front of flowers.

>   REPORTER 1
>   One pipeline official stated
>   that they hadn't seen so many
>   fossils . . .

INT. BASEMENT TV ROOM — CONTINUOUS

An oil pipeline is being constructed.

>   REPORTER 1
>   . . . in one place since they
>   ruptured a pipeline in Alberta
>   last year.

INT. FLOWER SHOP — DAY

The TV is on, and a commercial airline plane roars overhead.

>   REPORTER 2
>   In a related story, rogue
>   climate protesters began
>   picketing the . . .

INT. LIVING ROOM — CONTINUOUS

ON A RADIO

                    REPORTER 2
            . . . Vancouver Airport when
            they discovered airlines were
            jacking the cost of their
            tickets to . . .

ON A BASEMENT TV ROOM — Another climate protest is underway.

                    REPORTER 2
            . . . destinations planning a
            climate protest.

INT. INDUSTRIAL SHOP — CONTINUOUS

The same report continues on the radio.

                    REPORTER 2
            Airline officials stated that
            the increased demand allowed
            them to raise prices.

AUDIO STATIC, TV COLOUR BARS SPAGHETTI AND DISAPPEAR

INT. KITCHEN — DAY

A woman is watching the news on her laptop.

ON THE SCREEN — A reporter is on the street near Burnaby Mountain, updating the public on a pipeline protest.

                    REPORTER 3
          Things got heated today as
          police began to take down the
          phone numbers of protesters on
          Burnaby Mountain just behind
          these trees.

INT. POWDER ROOM — CONTINUOUS

A laptop is sitting next to the sink.

                    REPORTER 3
          When asked why they were
          recording phone numbers, one
          officer said that they were
          trying to reduce their carbon
          footprint by not transporting
          prisoners in paddy wagons.

EXT. GARDEN — CONTINUOUS

A woman is sitting at a table, watching the BS Northwest News on a laptop.

                    REPORTER 4
          Instead, protesters will be
          contacted later about their
          court hearings. The officer
          also said they hoped the
          protesters would take a greener
          method of transport and ride
          their bikes or walk to their
          court hearings.

INT. CABIN — CONTINUOUS

A family is watching the news on TV. The reporter is standing in front of an oil tank farm in Burnaby.

> REPORTER 3
> In other news, the Energy Board concluded its hearings on the northern oil pipeline today. There was a lot of talk, but not much was accomplished, apparently. One delegate said there was a lot of blah, blah, blah in the testimony.

AUDIO STATIC, TV COLOUR BARS SPAGHETTI AND DISAPPEAR

INTRO ANIMATION

A slick graphic blends images and geometric shapes, then wraps around to reveal the title: *Pressure Point*.

AUDIO STATIC, TV COLOUR BARS SPAGHETTI AND DISAPPEAR

INT. PRESSURE POINT STUDIO — DAY

The host, Francis von Zoofendorfen, looks into camera.

VON ZOOFENDORFEN
Hello and welcome to *Pressure Point*. I'm your host, Francis von Zoofendorfen. And joining me today is none other than the Minister of Energy. Well, hello, Minister of Energy, Roberto Gonzelezz. Welcome to the show!

GONZELEZZ
It's a pleasure! My friends call me Birdy.

VON ZOOFENDORFEN
Ah, well then, Roberto. Ah, why don't we just jump right in? Pipeline projects are being targeted by activists all across North America. And if I may suggest, the escalating protests are a thorn in the side of any government. Now, I've been told one of the reasons for the protests here is there is a perception that the hearings before the Energy Board are a sham.

                    GONZELEZZ
¿Qué hijo de perra le dijo eso?

(What son of a bitch told you that?)

¿Qué porquería es esa?

(What shit is that?)

Qué tontería.

(Rubbish.)

No lo creo.

(I don't believe it.)

A sham?

                    VON ZOOFENDORFEN
Ok, so, so what you are saying, ah, is that the evidence of submissions that are presented at the hearings could actually stop the project?

                    GONZELEZZ
But, ah . . . nada.

                    VON ZOOFENDORFEN
Nada?

                    GONZELEZZ
No.

                    VON ZOOFENDORFEN
No?

                    GONZELEZZ
No. The purpose of the hearings
is, one, to fine-tune the
project. Two, make sure there
is a project, and C, to, you
know, protect the freakin'
environment.

                    VON ZOOFENDORFEN
Multiple choice. C, protect the
freakin' environment?

                    GONZELEZZ
¡Sí!

                    VON ZOOFENDORFEN
Ha ha. Yes! Ok, then, well.

BACK TO VON ZOOFENDORFEN

                    VON ZOOFENDORFEN
Doesn't the fact that everyone
on the government side of
the hearings is from or has
connections to the energy
sector constitute a bias—

GONZELEZZ
—A bias toward what?

VON ZOOFENDORFEN
Oh, ah, easy, easy, lemon-squeezy. Let me finish.

GONZELEZZ
Sure. Go ahead.

VON ZOOFENDORFEN
There is a general perception among the public that the process is slanted to a foregone conclusion.

GONZELEZZ
Ok, ok, ok, ok, ok. Bias, eh? Slanted, a sham. What? The next thing you're going to say is it's rigged.

VON ZOOFENDORFEN
Oh, you said that. Not me. Ha! But is it true, though, that there are, are no environmentalists on the board?

GONZELEZZ
Well, A, it would make no sense to have an environmentalista on the board.

VON ZOOFENDORFEN
Well, why not?

GONZELEZZ
B, estupidas environmentalistas don't know a thing about energy.

VON ZOOFENDORFEN
Estupidas environmentalistas? What is that exactly, stupido?

GONZELEZZ
You know, these, these hippies in tuxedos on the board.

VON ZOOFENDORFEN
Oh, ok. Well, ok, maybe they aren't well dressed, but you have to admit, they tend to know a lot about the impact of energy on the environment.

GONZELEZZ
Well, C, they have tontas theories.

VON ZOOFENDORFEN
Again, wow. Ok, what does that mean? Tontas theories.

Gonzelezz hesitates, searches for the words.

GONZELEZZ
Tons of theories. Tons of theories.

VON ZOOFENDORFEN
Right. Ok. So.

BACK TO VON ZOOFENDORFEN

VON ZOOFENDORFEN
Ok. What is the purpose of the hearings then?

GONZELEZZ
The purpose of the hearings was to fulfill a regulatory requirement.

VON ZOOFENDORFEN
Huh. Hmmm.

GONZELEZZ
Ah, it's, it's basically, it's like a town hall meeting. And to distribute our terrific multiple choice surveys.

VON ZOOFENDORFEN
That is wonderful. So the real reason for these hearings was just to fulfill a regulatory
(MORE)

VON ZOOFENDORFEN (CONT'D)
requirement. And your main goal was to distribute a questionnaire. So the hearings really are just a formality.

GONZELEZZ
A. Not exactly a formality.

VON ZOOFENDORFEN
Ok, then, what is it then?

GONZELEZZ
Well, B. It's, ah, we are required to listen to everyone prattle on and on and on and on about their heartfelt thoughts and concerns.

VON ZOOFENDORFEN
I'm sorry . . . Prattle on?

GONZELEZZ
Yes. You know. Blah, blah, blah. We've heard it all before. Blah, blah, environment. Blah, blah, climate change. Honestly, it's quite tedious.

VON ZOOFENDORFEN
I'm going to be honest. It doesn't sound like you're taking any of the testimony seriously.

Gonzelezz gets angry.

GONZELEZZ
One, I am very, eh, serious.

VON ZOOFENDORFEN
Ok.

GONZELEZZ
And two, it's within our terms of reference to acknowledge everyone's prattling and to seriously consider it.
(under his breath)
Or not.

VON ZOOFENDORFEN
And you've considered all the opinions presented.

At first, quietly. Then loudly.

GONZELEZZ
Yes. And rejected them. Yes, it was all stupid nonsense, just as I suspected. And three, they
(MORE)

                    GONZELEZZ (CONT'D)
didn't answer our questions correctly. But we listened to all their, eh, stupid excuses and do-gooder ideas.

                    VON ZOOFENDORFEN
Ok, well, we're going to move along. Let me ask you this. One of the concerns is that there will be an oil spill.

                    GONZELEZZ
Yes, concerns are part of our mandate.

                    VON ZOOFENDORFEN
Ok, but, ah, what about the oil spill?

                    GONZELEZZ
A, that is not part of our mandate. One, we are to take, eh, people's thoughts and concerns and acknowledge them seriously. Two, oil spills are not our concern. C, fish are not our concern. And four, only concerns are our concern.

VON ZOOFENDORFEN
But, wait, isn't concerns about an oil spill the point of the hearings, though?

GONZELEZZ
A, well, but, but, yes, we will acknowledge the concerns, take them seriously and . . . Ok, fish.

VON ZOOFENDORFEN
But, when you say "we," what do you mean by "we"?

GONZELEZZ
The industry. Um, ahhh, the government.

VON ZOOFENDORFEN
Wait . . . What is it, the government or industry?

Gonzelezz looks a bit sheepish.

GONZELEZZ
We, um, it's the same thing.

VON ZOOFENDORFEN
But, hold on, you are part of the government, right? Shouldn't you be recommending that we protect fish from oil spills?

GONZELEZZ
¿Yo? Me?

VON ZOOFENDORFEN
Yes, you. Birdy . . .

GONZELEZZ
Me personally?

VON ZOOFENDORFEN
Birdy protects the fish. Now that, whoa, that would be quite the thing. Birdy is responsible for protecting the fish.

GONZELEZZ
One, personally? No, no, no, no, no, no, no.

VON ZOOFENDORFEN
No?

GONZELEZZ
No, but if, ah, they bring, ah, if industry brought a project to us, we could recommended it to Cabinet. We, the collective "we."

VON ZOOFENDORFEN
I see. The collective "we." And did you recommend, as a board, any changes to this project to protect the environment?

GONZELEZZ
Ah, no, because there was a general mood to reduce the red tape.

VON ZOOFENDORFEN
Red tape. So when you say red tape, what exactly do you mean by red tape?

GONZELEZZ
Well, A, I've never actually seen the red tape myself. B, but I've heard a lot about it and I do understand it's nasty, nasty stuff. C, it sticks to everything. And D, it's terrible, terrible stuff.

VON ZOOFENDORFEN
Ok, and who told you that? Was it a survey expert or—

GONZELEZZ
—The industry.

VON ZOOFENDORFEN
Ah, ok, I see. All right, well. So, what about the fish?

GONZELEZZ
The few fish of concern were, well, A, of little value. Hey, look, I have silverfish in my kitchen all the time, and they are a nuisance.

VON ZOOFENDORFEN
Ok. I think we are talking about fish in streams and lakes?

Gonzelezz gets excited.

GONZELEZZ
Well, no one is catching or selling these fish affected by this project. I mean, they aren't even being used in fish tanks. So they are pretty much worthless.

VON ZOOFENDORFEN
Ok, well, all right. Ok, another thing the public is concerned about is that if there is a spill, the taxpayer will get stuck with most of the clean-up costs.

GONZELEZZ
Yes, that's terrible. Whoo-hoo.

VON ZOOFENDORFEN
What is terrible?

GONZELEZZ
It's really just terrible.

VON ZOOFENDORFEN
Ok, all right. And you don't see any injustice in that whatsoever?

GONZELEZZ
Nada. Not really. A, it would be a greater injustice if any shareholders were impacted because of our policies, you know. B, that would be very, very terrible. Three, it would be super, super terrible.

VON ZOOFENDORFEN
And you don't have any suggestions regarding this?

GONZELEZZ
Yes. A, the taxpayers that are concerned about this project causing higher taxes should buy shares in the oil companies to offset their higher taxes, you see. Two, then when the spill happens they will feel much better about it. C, and that's half the battle to acknowledging and alleviating concerns.

VON ZOOFENDORFEN
Elevating?

GONZELEZZ
Alleviates. It alleviates these issues.

VON ZOOFENDORFEN
So effectively you acknowledge there will be a spill?

GONZELEZZ
Effectively, eventually. Kinda the same thing. It would be delusional to think that there
(MORE)

GONZELEZZ (CONT'D)
wouldn't be an oil spill at some point. Oil spills happen all the time. I've got one in my driveway from my own car. It's part of the natural ecosystem.

VON ZOOFENDORFEN
What about the impact on First Nations people and their communities?

GONZELEZZ
They should do the same. Buy shares. At least then they can profit for when we ruin, maybe not ruin, but make their communities less tranquil and livable than they would like. And then they would have the money to move away.

VON ZOOFENDORFEN
I'm sure that would resonate well with Nations that have lived in the same place for millennia.

GONZELEZZ
Well, let's just say we all have to be adaptable.

VON ZOOFENDORFEN
So, ordinary citizens, either through their taxes or by getting out of the way, should bear the brunt for all externalities inflicted upon them by this project. Is that what I'm hearing?

GONZELEZZ
Isn't capitalism wonderful?

VON ZOOFENDORFEN
It is?

GONZELEZZ
The public pays for everything.

VON ZOOFENDORFEN
That's not—

GONZELEZZ
—Canada is such a kind and caring country!

VON ZOOFENDORFEN
Ok, um, so you don't think the companies themselves should pay for any clean-up whatsoever?

Gonzelezz laughs.

> **GONZELEZZ**
> Oh, gosh, no. No, no, no, no, no, no, no. One, you see, this would drive down share prices. Can't do that at all. I mean, ultimately this could even affect the Canada Pension Plan.

He leans forward and von Zoofendorfen leans back.

> **GONZELEZZ**
> B. This is a bad idea! This is a very bad idea!

> **VON ZOOFENDORFEN**
> I see you are very passionate about this point.

> **GONZELEZZ**
> I'm very, very passionate. Yes. I care.

> **VON ZOOFENDORFEN**
> I can see that.

> **GONZELEZZ**
> I care about the energy.

VON ZOOFENDORFEN
Ah, but, here's the question I have. So, setting aside some of the revenue to fund a disaster response, that is not the answer in your view?

GONZELEZZ
Well, it would negate the whole purpose of the exercise, my friend.

VON ZOOFENDORFEN
Ok, maybe that is the concern.

GONZELEZZ
I think you're catching on.

VON ZOOFENDORFEN
I am?

GONZELEZZ
One, it's about acknowledging the concerns. B, oil spills are not our concerns. C, fish are not our concern. D, only concerns are our concerns. I already told you about these concerns.

VON ZOOFENDORFEN
Oh, ok, well . . .

                    GONZELEZZ
          But C, now you are
          acknowledging concerns.

                    VON ZOOFENDORFEN
          I—

                    GONZELEZZ
          —You see?

                    VON ZOOFENDORFEN
          Yeah.

                    GONZELEZZ
          You see.

Gonzelezz smacks von Zoofendorfen's knee. Von
Zoofendorfen winces.

                    VON ZOOFENDORFEN
          Ok, that . . . hurt.

                    GONZELEZZ
          Now you're catching on.

                    VON ZOOFENDORFEN
          Listen, just to refocus, for
          me, the only thing the industry
          is really willing to give is
          advice.

Gonzelezz nods his head in the affirmative.

                    GONZELEZZ
          A, you see I'm acknowledging,
          you see, you see. So, it's
          about you demonstrate that you
          are taking in these concerns.
          And B, advice, ah, is kind of a
          grey area.

                    VON ZOOFENDORFEN
          Ok, so what I'm getting from
          this is these hearings are just
          a public relations exercise.

Gonzelezz points at him.

                    GONZELEZZ
          Well, public relations, public
          consultation. A, it's six of
          one and eight of the other, you
          know. It's, it's as long as we
          are acknowledging concerns and
          really listening to people's
          thoughts and concerns.

                    VON ZOOFENDORFEN
          Yes.

Gonzelezz looks self-righteously sincere.

                    GONZELEZZ
          And then we go ahead and do
          what we were going to do in the
          first place.

VON ZOOFENDORFEN
Well, ok, I'm glad you cleared that up.

They laugh.

GONZELEZZ
I'm always happy to acknowledge your concerns.

VON ZOOFENDORFEN
Well, ok, and that's much appreciated, and A, thank you for being here.

GONZELEZZ
B, always happy to listen.
        (under his breath)
But that's about all.

VON ZOOFENDORFEN
Ok, all right. And C. Thank you for being here.

GONZELEZZ
C, you later.

VON ZOOFENDORFEN
Ok, wow! I may need an escort to my car after this.

GONZELEZZ
Eh, C what I did there?

                    VON ZOOFENDORFEN
          Ah, no what?

Gonzelezz laughs and looks for his assistant.

                    GONZELEZZ
          C you later!

                    VON ZOOFENDORFEN
          And D, lightful, speaking with
          you, Birdy, Minister of Energy.
          You've been a treat and wow,
          folks, we are out of time. I
          am your host, Francis von
          Zoofendorfen and this—

                    GONZELEZZ
          —Hey!

                    VON ZOOFENDORFEN
          Hello.

                    GONZELEZZ
          C me now, C me later.

Gonzelezz laughs, gets up and leaves.

                    VON ZOOFENDORFEN
          Ok, he's off. Ladies and
          gentlemen, this has been
          Pressure Point. And I'm your
          host, Francis von Zoofendorfen.

Thanks for watching! C you next time.

GONZELEZZ (O.S.)
A, you are right. B, good at listening. C-ing is hearing and four-tunate to get out of here. Bye!

FADE TO:

EXT. VANCOUVER SKY (DRONE) — NIGHT

Fireworks explode into the night sky and we . . .

FADE OUT

EPISODE 6:

The Fine Art of Sustainable Clear-Cuts

Ryan Cowie plays Jack Trade, the Minister of Forestry and the Minister of the Environment, aka the Minister of Two Pseudo Green Hats.

192.

                    ANNOUNCER
          Warning. Hyper-sensitive,
          serious and easily offended
          viewers and politicians may
          find that some dialogue will
          make them laugh. Consult your
          physician before consuming this
          content.

AUDIO STATIC, TV COLOUR BARS SPAGHETTI AND DISAPPEAR

EXT. VANCOUVER CITY (AERIAL) — NIGHT

A brilliant shot of the downtown core all lit up.

                    VON ZOOFENDORFEN
          It's time for *Pressure Point*.
          Here's what people have been
          watching and hearing in the
          news this week.

EXT. PARK BENCH — DAY

OVER THE SHOULDER — of a man reading the *Northern Comment* newspaper. The headline reads: "Province Celebrates 28th Anniversary of War of the Woods Protest."

The man is reading aloud.

> MAN READING NEWSPAPER
> Hey, guys, listen to this. The Province is celebrating the 28th anniversary of the Clayoquot Sound protest known as the War of the Woods.

INT. HOME OFFICE — MOMENTS LATER

An old 4 × 3 TV is perched on a bookshelf. A clip of the protest is playing.

> MAN READING NEWSPAPER
> Protesters tried to stop the clear-cutting of virgin old-growth trees and 857 people were arrested.

BACK TO MAN

> MAN READING NEWSPAPER
> In spite of the protest, the forest was still cut down.

INT. OFFICE — DAY

A modern protest is underway and being broadcast on a desktop TV.

                    MAN READING NEWSPAPER
               What are they celebrating? How
               many people were arrested or
               that they cut down the woods?

AUDIO STATIC, TV COLOUR BARS SPAGHETTI AND
DISAPPEAR

INT. OLD RUSTIC HOUSE — DAY

A vintage phone and radio take up real estate
on the small kitchen table. A report about
the protest is playing on the radio.

                         REPORTER 1
               Protesters marched through
               downtown Vancouver today . . .

INT. ANOTHER HOUSE — CONTINUOUS

A radio is on the kitchen table. The report
about the protest blares out.

                         REPORTER 1
               . . . over what they say
               is another assault on the
               remaining old-growth forests.

INT. WORKSHOP — CONTINUOUS

A small radio shows the time, 5:39 PM, on the
display.

195.

                    REPORTER 1
          Police were seen using
          the jaws of life to remove
          protesters who had chained
          themselves . . .

INT. STORE — CONTINUOUS

A ghetto blaster is on a stand.

                    REPORTER 1
          . . . to cherry blossom trees
          lining Hornby Street.

AUDIO STATIC, TV COLOUR BARS SPAGHETTI AND DISAPPEAR

INT. BARBERSHOP — DAY

A TV screen hanging from the ceiling keeps customers in the loop with the daily news. A beautiful cherry blossom tree is on display in the report in progress.

ON THE REPORTER — standing on a street full of cherry blossom trees.

                    REPORTER 2
          Protesters say they targeted
          the cherry blossom tree because
          of its symbolic and valuable
                      (MORE)

                    REPORTER 2 (CONT'D)
          wood. Environmentalists
          watching the protest commented
          that protesters should have
          directed their attention to
          wild wood rather than urban
          wood.

INT. HOME DINING ROOM - CONTINUOUS

An old man, Tom Renyard, is watching the news on his laptop.

                    REPORTER 2
          Protesters responded that a
          protest in the bush seen by no
          one is not a protest at all.

INT. DOCTOR'S WAITING ROOM - CONTINUOUS

                    REPORTER 2
          It is a collection of nature
          lovers chained to random trees.

AUDIO STATIC, TV COLOUR BARS SPAGHETTI AND DISAPPEAR

INT. BEDROOM - DAY

On the TV hanging on a wall the news is doing a story about deforestation. An aerial shot of clear-cut forests is on the screen, then . . .

A Green Channel reporter stands among some trees.

>   REPORTER 3
> Deforestation rages across
> the world, and large swaths of
> land that were once covered in
> forests . . .

A tractor drives past a large field of corn.

>   REPORTER 3
> . . . are now considered net
> carbon emitters. Forests
> are supposed to be carbon
> sinks . . .

BACK TO THE REPORTER

>   REPORTER 3
> . . . but these days the only
> sinks politicians seem to care
> about . . .

ON A RADIO — next to a kitchen sink.

>   REPORTER 3
> . . . are kitchen sinks,

INT. BASEMENT KITCHEN — CONTINUOUS

PANNING OVER — to a radio on the counter and we realize the story is on the radio.

                    REPORTER 3
          . . . where they prepare food,
          that was grown on land,

EXT. BACKYARD — CONTINUOUS

The same report is coming through a laptop sitting on a picnic table.

                    REPORTER 3
          . . . that was once a carbon
          sink forest.

AUDIO STATIC, TV COLOUR BARS SPAGHETTI AND DISAPPEAR

INTRO ANIMATION

A slick graphic blends images and geometric shapes, then wraps around to reveal the title: *Pressure Point*.

AUDIO STATIC, TV COLOUR BARS SPAGHETTI AND DISAPPEAR

INT. PRESSURE POINT STUDIO — DAY

The host, Francis von Zoofendorfen, looks into camera.

          VON ZOOFENDORFEN
    Hello and welcome to *Pressure Point*.

ON VON ZOOFENDORFEN'S GUEST — he's distracted and checking his nails.

          VON ZOOFENDORFEN (O.S)
    I'm your host, Francis von Zoofendorfen.

WIDER — the angle reveals both the host and the guest, Jack Trade.

          VON ZOOFENDORFEN
    Joining me is none other than Jack Trade, the minister of two portfolios.

WIDER — they are both in shot.

          VON ZOOFENDORFEN
    You are head of the Ministry of Forestry and the Ministry of the Environment. Welcome to the show, Minister and Minister.

INTERCUT BETWEEN THEM

              TRADE
Thank you! It's a pleasure for both of us to be here.

Trade chuckles at their corny joke.

           VON ZOOFENDORFEN
And by the way, before I forget to say it, congratulations to the both of you for achieving what so few have done.

              TRADE
Thanks! It's a pleasure to serve the people times two.

           VON ZOOFENDORFEN
Now, Ministers Trade, some would say that you represent two portfolios with diametrically opposing goals. One is about saving trees while the other is about cutting the trees down.

Trade nods his head as if he's answering for two different people.

              TRADE
Yes. And yes.

VON ZOOFENDORFEN
Well, ok then, so,

BACK TO VON ZOOFENDORFEN

VON ZOOFENDORFEN
. . . tell me, how do you manage those conflicting concepts?

TRADE
Yes, well, frankly speaking,

Trade points at the nipple area on the left side of his chest and then the right side.

TRADE
. . . we don't see them as opposing goals. Some trees need to be cut down to make room for other trees.

VON ZOOFENDORFEN
Oh. Really?

TRADE
Well, yes, as the old saying goes, I can see the forest for the wood.

Trade smirks at his twist on the old saying.

                    TRADE
I mean, trees.

                VON ZOOFENDORFEN
Ah, yes, you got me.

BACK TO VON ZOOFENDORFEN

                    TRADE
I like to joke.

                VON ZOOFENDORFEN
That's so healthy, to joke. As
long as our management of the
forests isn't a joke in the
end.

                    TRADE
Precisely.

                VON ZOOFENDORFEN
Speaking of precisely,

WIDER

                VON ZOOFENDORFEN
. . . I'm sure you and the
provincial Treasury both see
the wood. Everybody wants wood.
Except those that don't.

                    TRADE
Wood is good.

                    VON ZOOFENDORFEN
Oh, that is good. That is good
that wood is good.

                    TRADE
Could be a slogan.

                    VON ZOOFENDORFEN
Yes, a very good slogan. You
should write that down.

Trade types it into his phone.

                    TRADE
Frankly speaking, making trees
is a very complicated business.

                    VON ZOOFENDORFEN
Ok, and how did you get to be
involved in this complicated
business, as you call it?

                    TRADE
Well, when the Premier of
British Columbia calls you to
do something, you do it.

                    VON ZOOFENDORFEN
You do, do you?

TRADE
          Absolutely. I'm a team player.
          There's no "I" in team.

                    VON ZOOFENDORFEN
          Holy sweet jumping grasshopper,
          you are on a roll, sir. You
          should write that down. That is
          a good one as well.

Trade madly types this into his phone as well.

                    VON ZOOFENDORFEN
          Wood is good. And there is no
          "I" in team. You are a slogan
          machine.

BACK TO VON ZOOFENDORFEN

                    VON ZOOFENDORFEN
          Here's the issue that was
          brought to me. And that is
          this. The public seems to feel
          that your government is pro-
          development and pro-industry.

Trade bobs back and forth, looking skeptical.

                    VON ZOOFENDORFEN
          So, I ask you, is the
          environment . . .

BACK TO VON ZOOFENDORFEN

                    VON ZOOFENDORFEN
          . . . being short-changed?
          Not only by your government's
          general stance, but by the fact
          that you, a very seemingly,
          very pro-industry minister,
          are also representing the
          Environment Ministry at the
          same time.

                    TRADE
          Well, yes, that's a good
          question.

He points at the left and right sides of his
chest again.

                    TRADE
          But we see our jobs as making
          sure our forest is sustainable.

                    VON ZOOFENDORFEN
          Ok, so what does that mean to
          you?

                    TRADE
          Well, we always want a steady
          supply of trees to cut down to
          turn into products which thereby
                    (MORE)

TRADE (CONT'D)
creates jobs, jobs, jobs and
more jobs, helping keep the
economy sustainable.

VON ZOOFENDORFEN
So, to you, sustainability
means keeping a sustainable
economy?

TRADE
Yes. Something like that.

VON ZOOFENDORFEN
So, for you, sustainability
really doesn't refer at all
to creating a sustainable
environment?

TRADE
Not true. But not false.

VON ZOOFENDORFEN
Ok, how about half-true?

Trade shrugs and nods, then breaks into a sheepish grin.

VON ZOOFENDORFEN
Ok, here's the thing. But if
you are thinking only about the
(MORE)

VON ZOOFENDORFEN (CONT'D)
economy, are you really able
to only just think about the
environment for its own sake?

Von Zoofendorfen meshes his fingers together, slightly agitated.

TRADE
Look, the environment can
take care of itself. It really
doesn't need much hand-holding
from the government. The trees
will grow, and we help them
along with planting programs
and such and such. And we
simply don't take too much wood
at once. Take what you need,
not what you want. That's my
motto, even if they amount to
the same thing in the end.

VON ZOOFENDORFEN
Oh! So need and want are the
same thing. Sounds pretty
greedy to me.

TRADE
Perhaps. But there is no
company that wants to ruin
their supply chain. It's not
logical.

                    VON ZOOFENDORFEN
No.

                    TRADE
It's simply not logical.

                    VON ZOOFENDORFEN
It's not? What about the notion that once the opportunity is over, the executives move onto something else, so there is no incentive to make any venture sustainable?

                    TRADE
I think that's just a theory.

                    VON ZOOFENDORFEN
A theory?

                    TRADE
Yes, something like that.

ON VON ZOOFENDORFEN

                    VON ZOOFENDORFEN
So, ok, do you have some kind of formula to determine how much wood to take? And who gets to take what?

TRADE
Yes. Whoever contributes the most to the party.

Trade is oblivious that he's slipped up.

VON ZOOFENDORFEN
Wait, I'm sorry, did you say the party?

TRADE
Sorry, tax base.

VON ZOOFENDORFEN
So the Government is just interested in maximizing the tax base?

TRADE
You could say that.

VON ZOOFENDORFEN
So what species of trees are you more interested, as a government, in cutting down to improve the tax base? Cedar, Douglas Fir, Pine or Poplar? Bearing in mind the splinters, of course.

                    TRADE
          Whatever is poplar at the
          moment.

He smirks at yet another corny joke.

                    VON ZOOFENDORFEN
          Ha! You're just full of them,
          aren't you? Seriously, you must
          have some guiding principle
          when it comes to which trees to
          cut down.

                    TRADE
          Actually, we tend to avoid
          nots.

                    VON ZOOFENDORFEN
          Knots in the wood?

                    TRADE
          No, nots as in not harvesting.
          We have a harvest mandate
          generally.

                    VON ZOOFENDORFEN
          Ok, I see—

                    TRADE
          —And we work with the forest
          companies to determine the rate
          of harvest.

VON ZOOFENDORFEN
What do you mean by "work with"?

TRADE
They tell us what they want to do.

VON ZOOFENDORFEN
Ok, so you don't independently determine what the appropriate level of harvest is?

TRADE
Hell no! No, no. Our motto is, ah, to work smarter, not harder.

VON ZOOFENDORFEN
So for you, working smarter is just winging it?

TRADE
Precisely. Sometimes intuition is our best friend.

VON ZOOFENDORFEN
Wow. Ok. So what do the companies typically say?

TRADE
Less is more.

VON ZOOFENDORFEN
Don't let anyone tell you that you don't know all the clichés. You've got them nailed down.

Trade beams.

VON ZOOFENDORFEN
So they say cutting less results in higher prices?

TRADE
No. Less talking results in less problems with the public and more profits.

VON ZOOFENDORFEN
So they don't tell you anything?

TRADE
Well, that's private information.

VON ZOOFENDORFEN
Ok, well, I suppose, but we are talking about public trees, public land, public things . . . So, how is that private?

                    TRADE
          Well, the forest companies,
          very good people I might add
          who contribute a lot to the
          party, ur, government coffers,
          would not want us to reveal
          their methods because it might
          have an impact on their bottom
          line. And nothing is worse than
          having an impact on your bottom
          line.

                    VON ZOOFENDORFEN
          Oh my goodness. Yes, no one
          wants their bottom line
          impacted unless it's a really
          good impact.

Von Zoofendorfen shifts in his seat to
indicate a slight discomfort at the thought
of bottom-line impacts and then changes his
line of questioning.

                    VON ZOOFENDORFEN
          But shouldn't the public
          know and approve of the rate
          of harvest of their public
          forests?

                    TRADE
          Actually, wood is very
          complicated.

                    VON ZOOFENDORFEN
          It is?

                    TRADE
          Yeah.

                    VON ZOOFENDORFEN
          Ok.

Trade chuckles.

                    VON ZOOFENDORFEN
          Tell my viewers, how is wood
          complicated?

                    TRADE
          I will be honest.

                    VON ZOOFENDORFEN
          Please.

                    TRADE
          Well, frankly speaking, and I
          like to be honest about this,
          the rate of harvest has to
          do with the circumference of
          timbers on an individual basis,
          and how that on a volume of a
          pile of logs basis will flow
          through the entire processing
          chain and then go as quickly
                    (MORE)

TRADE (CONT'D)
out of the country, on that basis. So you can see there is a lot to it.

VON ZOOFENDORFEN
I've got to be honest with you. That sounds like a lot of gibberish.

TRADE
It does to me too. I told you it was complicated.

VON ZOOFENDORFEN
It sounds to me like you're trying to greenwash the whole process.

TRADE
Just the so-called parks that need it. It's so, so complicated we have to gloss over the details or we all get confused.

VON ZOOFENDORFEN
Correct me if I'm wrong, but basically it sounds like to me that we take these raw logs, we ship them off to someone else
(MORE)

VON ZOOFENDORFEN (CONT'D)
for pennies. Then, they take these raw logs and do a whole bunch of things to them and turn them into finished or semi-finished products. Then Canadians buy back these products for something like 50 times more than we sold the wood for. Is that how it works?

TRADE
Something like that.

VON ZOOFENDORFEN
And that's good for us?

TRADE
Well, it might not be good for you and me, mostly you. But that's not the point. It's good for the economy. The economy is what counts.

Trade makes a sweeping gesture with his hands, suggesting a large, global picture.

VON ZOOFENDORFEN
Can the public see the books on this?

                    TRADE
Ah, no.

                VON ZOOFENDORFEN
No. Ok. Why is that?

                    TRADE
Well, it's private information
that I'm not obliged, I mean,
able to divulge.

                VON ZOOFENDORFEN
All right. I'm gonna be very
honest here, Jack. May I call
you Jack? Or would you prefer
Minister Wood Trader?

                    TRADE
Jack of All Trades works for
me.

                VON ZOOFENDORFEN
Ah, ok. Jack of Many Bad
Trades. All right, so. Jack.
I'm going to be honest. I've
heard this line before from
your government, and the
public is not happy about
how our forests are seemingly
evaporating before our eyes.
Let's switch it up. Let me ask
you this—

                    TRADE
          —No.

                    VON ZOOFENDORFEN
          No?

                    TRADE
          I was just kidding.

                    VON ZOOFENDORFEN
          Ah, you got me, right there.

Von Zoofendorfen leans in. Then Trade leans in and whispers.

                    TRADE
          What do you need to know?

                    VON ZOOFENDORFEN
          I was told by a friend that in
          Japan they have no plans for
          cutting down their trees in the
          near future. Do you know why?

                    TRADE
          No.

                    VON ZOOFENDORFEN
          He said that as long as Canada
          plans on giving away its trees,
          there is no point in cutting
          down theirs. What do you say to
          that?

                    TRADE
          Sounds like Canada is being
          pretty competitive.

                    VON ZOOFENDORFEN
          Or foolish.

                    TRADE
          Same thing. The important thing
          is, our wood is getting market
          share. And market share is hard
          to get. Even if it costs us
          money to do it.

                    VON ZOOFENDORFEN
          If we're losing money, what's
          the point of cutting them down?
          Ok, let's be hypothetical for a
          moment.

Trade sits back in his chair.

                    TRADE
          Oooh, geez . . . Here it comes,
          the hypotheticals . . .
              (he strings together a few rhyming words)
                . . . the parentheticals, the
          highly ethicals, and the
          vaguely hypotheticals.

VON ZOOFENDORFEN
Yes, the hypotheticals. Let's say it takes 200 years to grow a tree to maturity. For that group of trees to be sustainable, so you never run out of trees, you can only take one 200th of those trees in a given forest per year. Correct?

TRADE
Statistically, statistics are not my strong point. Ah, 60% of the time, I'm up to 100% of the time wrong.

VON ZOOFENDORFEN
This is simple math. We're talking basic fractions here.

TRADE
Nothin's worse than fractions. Sorry. Not good with fractions either. Or other types of mathology.

VON ZOOFENDORFEN
But you run two ministries.

TRADE
Ministry math I can do. I'm running two, most, if not all, of the time.

VON ZOOFENDORFEN
Ok, yes, that's why you are on the show. Wow. Ok.

TRADE
Both of us are on the show.

VON ZOOFENDORFEN
Well, physically, yes. We are both on the show.

Von Zoofendorfen laughs.

VON ZOOFENDORFEN
Basically what that means is to have the forest completely sustainable, you would have to take 200 years to cut all the trees down. You would need a 200-year rotation. And we are cutting trees down way faster than that. It's that simple.

TRADE
Sorry, I don't like to rotate. It makes me dizzy.

VON ZOOFENDORFEN
This whole idea that we have to cut our trees down so fast makes me and the public dizzy.

Trade pulls a packet of pills out of his pocket.

>TRADE
>Can I offer you a little opioid? It's way better than a bunch of useless trees, and you won't be bothered about anything. They sure help with dizziness, and they're one of our best imports at the moment.

>VON ZOOFENDORFEN
>Pass.

>TRADE
>Sure?

>VON ZOOFENDORFEN
>Positive. How about this? One report said that Canada disturbs more virgin forest each year than any other country in the world. I have to be honest, Minister and Minister, that doesn't sound sustainable to me at all.

>TRADE
>It depends on what you mean by "disturb."

VON ZOOFENDORFEN
Well, how about this? I am disturbed that we are cutting down the trees . . . way too fast!

TRADE
That's not disturbing, that's harvesting. Two totally different matters.

VON ZOOFENDORFEN
Ok, well, you say tomayto, some say tomahto. And I say, crapola.

TRADE
Sure, there's all kinds of fake news out there. And there's all kinds of that surrounding the cutting of trees. So you can pretty much believe everything you read these days—

Von Zoofendorfen interrupts.

VON ZOOFENDORFEN
—You mean "can't."

TRADE
. . . especially when it's coming from your government. We have a great propaganda, ur, information, program that explains in much greater detail how things were, how things are and how things will be.

VON ZOOFENDORFEN
Glad we cleared that up. Now. How would the public get this information? Leaflets, brochures, reports?

TRADE
Well, no, no, no. Not like that.
              (happily)
We've gone paperless so that we can save trees . . .
         (under his breath)
. . . for shipping.

VON ZOOFENDORFEN
Sorry. I didn't catch what you said.

TRADE
Just a little burble.

                    VON ZOOFENDORFEN
A burble?

                    TRADE
Yes. I didn't say "shipping," I
said "keeping."

                    VON ZOOFENDORFEN
Right. Ok. Do these reports
have any data, statistics,
perhaps? Some rock-solid
numbers that the public can
actually use?

                    TRADE
Well, I'm like a rock. You
won't get a statistic out of me.

He chuckles.

                    VON ZOOFENDORFEN
I believe you. I believe you
so much so that I think you
believe the public should just
blindly believe the folks in
power no matter what.

                    TRADE
But of course. All of us in
power have only the best of
intentions for all.

VON ZOOFENDORFEN
All for one, and one gets all.

TRADE
Yes, something like that. But maybe two is the best number.

VON ZOOFENDORFEN
Yes, two ministers, one decision-maker.

TRADE
I'm glad we agree on that basic bit of mathology.

VON ZOOFENDORFEN
This has been fruitless. Well, this has been a woody interview. And I believe we have reached its logical conclusion. So, I thank you, Minister, and I thank you, Minister.
(turning to camera)
And I thank you for watching. This has been *Pressure Point*. And I'm your host, Francis von Zoofendorfen. Until next time, have yourselves a beautiful morning, afternoon and or evening.

					TRADE
		Cameras off?

Von Zoofendorfen looks off the set.

					VON ZOOFENDORFEN
		Now, now the cameras are off.

Trade takes out his cellphone, moves away a bit, dials.

					TRADE
		Hello, Premier? I think I have
		another outlet that we need to
		muzzle.

He looks up and notices that von Zoofendorfen is listening.

ON VON ZOOFENDORFEN

					TRADE
		Ah, oh, I mean, we should look
		into their broadcast licence
		because there are probably some
		potential issues.

BACK TO TRADE

                    TRADE
              (Avoids eye contact)
          It has been a pleasure to be
          here.

                    VON ZOOFENDORFEN
          You are correct, it has been a
          pleasure. Or knot.

                                        FADE TO:

EXT. VANCOUVER SKY (DRONE) — NIGHT

Fireworks explode into the night sky and
we . . .

                                        FADE OUT

EPISODE 7:

The Poop Dilution Solution

Vivian Davidson plays Svetlana Poopanova, the Minister of Immigration and Free Trade, aka the Minister of Crappy Conspiracy Theories.

                    ANNOUNCER
          Warning. The following program
          contains rude, sassy, adult-
          themed, comical material.
          Easily offended viewers and
          politicians will find that
          some dialogue will make them
          chuckle and occasionally laugh
          out loud. Viewer discretion is
          perhaps advised.

AUDIO STATIC, TV COLOUR BARS SPAGHETTI AND
DISAPPEAR

EXT. VANCOUVER CITY (AERIAL) — NIGHT

A brilliant shot of the downtown core all
lit up.

                    VON ZOOFENDORFEN
          It's time for *Pressure Point*.
          Here's what people have been
          watching and hearing in the
          news this week.

AUDIO STATIC, TV COLOUR BARS SPAGHETTI AND
DISAPPEAR

INT. POLITICIAN'S OFFICE — DAY

The news is streaming on a laptop. Log booms
litter the shorelines of the Fraser River.

                    REPORTER 1
          The log dispute has been
          heating up again between Canada
          and the United States,

ON A WHITE RADIO — CONTINUOUS

                    REPORTER 1
          . . . with the US taking
          the position that Canada is
          breaking the NAFTA agreement by
          selling its logs below market
          price.

INT. GARAGE — MOMENTS LATER

A shop radio is perched on a high shelf.

                    REPORTER 1
          And the Americans also lodged a
          complaint . . .

INT. BEDROOM — CONTINUOUS

The TV is turned on to the news. We see a massive old-growth log on a logging truck.

                    REPORTER 1
          . . . that Canadian logs are
          undersized.

AUDIO STATIC, TV COLOUR BARS SPAGHETTI AND DISAPPEAR

INT. BEDROOM — DAY

The BS Northwest News is streaming. A reporter is live on the lawn of the BC legislature.

Superscript: January 2021

          REPORTER 2
    Political leaders are rejoicing today about the launch of a brand new treatment plant.

THE NEW TREATMENT PLANT — on the shore of the ocean.

          REPORTER 2
    Prior to today,

ON A CELLPHONE — streaming the same report.

          REPORTER 2
    . . . the Victoria area has been . . .

BACK TO REPORTER 2

234.

                    REPORTER 2
            . . . guilty of dumping raw
            sewage . . .

BACK TO CELLPHONE — a still of a sewage
outfall going into the ocean.

                    REPORTER 2
            . . . into the ocean since 1894.

INT. VIETNAMESE RESTAURANT — CONTINUOUS

The TV is on the wall above the till.

                    REPORTER 2
            British Columbians will no
            longer be the butt of American
            jokes as we will no longer be
            sending floaties across the
            ocean to American shorelines.

AUDIO STATIC, TV COLOUR BARS SPAGHETTI AND
DISAPPEAR

INT. CRAFT SHOP — DAY

A news report about high water on the Fraser
River is streaming on a tablet.

                    REPORTER 3
          Crap was seen floating down the
          Fraser River today after what
          is being described as a flood
          event like no other.

INT. CRAFT SHOP — CONTINUOUS

A desktop TV nestled between baskets of dried
flowers streams the same report. The muddy
Fraser water laps at the shoreline onscreen.

                    REPORTER 3
          The water was a frothy, brown
          slurry that sent scientists
          scrambling for their sampling
          kits.

AUDIO STATIC, TV COLOUR BARS SPAGHETTI AND
DISAPPEAR

EXT. GARDEN — DAY

A laptop on a picnic table streams a news
report featuring an image of West Vancouver.

                    REPORTER 4
          A sewage slick is making its
          way under the Lions Gate Bridge
          on its way along the north
          shore of Burrard Inlet right
                    (MORE)

                    REPORTER 4 (CONT'D)
          in front of expensive
          West Vancouver waterfront
          properties.

INT. NEIGHBOURHOOD PUB - DAY

A ceiling-mounted TV is tuned into The Green
Channel news report. A reporter is mid-story
and live on a Stanley Park beach with West
Vancouver in the background.

                    REPORTER 5
          One homeowner was heard saying
          that the whole issue is an
          attempt to crap all over the
          1% who have worked so hard
          for their multimillion dollar
          homes.

EXT. VICTORIA CLOVER POINT BEACH - DAY

Reporter 2 is reporting from a beach in
Victoria that is lined by houses overlooking
the ocean.

                    REPORTER 2
          The beaches near Clover Point
          and the nearby parks are closed
          today because the coliform
          count is 10 times the safe
          limit.

ON HOUSES — overlooking the ocean.

INT. INDIAN RESTAURANT — CONTINUOUS

The wall-mounted TV is tuned into the same Green Channel news report.

>REPORTER 2
> Officials are telling us that staff at the new treatment plant that now treats the Greater Victoria area sewage before it is released into the Juan de Fuca Strait . . .

INT. ARCHITECT'S OFFICE — CONTINUOUS

>REPORTER 2
> . . . are unable to explain the sudden appearance of, well, unprocessed floaties. Some are speculating that there was a breach in the system, but officials say that this isn't possible. The investigation continues.

INT. BARBER SHOP — DAY

Another sewage story is concluding on the shop's TV. A floatie can be seen in shallow water.

                    REPORTER 4
          The whole issue is a load of
          crap.

AUDIO STATIC, TV COLOUR BARS SPAGHETTI AND
DISAPPEAR

INTRO ANIMATION

A slick graphic blends images and geometric
shapes, then wraps around to reveal the
title: *Pressure Point*.

AUDIO STATIC, TV COLOUR BARS SPAGHETTI AND
DISAPPEAR

INT. PRESSURE POINT STUDIO — DAY

The host, Francis von Zoofendorfen, looks
into camera.

                  VON ZOOFENDORFEN
          Hello and welcome to *Pressure
          Point*. I'm your host, Francis
          von Zoofendorfen. And joining
          me today is the Minister of
          Immigration and Free Trade,
          Svetlana Poopanova. Minister
          Poopanova, welcome to the show.

                     POOPANOVA
          Pleasure to be here.

VON ZOOFENDORFEN
Ah, now, Svetlana, shall I call you Ms. Minister?

POOPANOVA
No. I want to keep it formal. You can call me Minister Poop—

VON ZOOFENDORFEN
—All right, then. Minister Poopie it is. Now, the sewage situation for the Greater Victoria area is back in the news. After 100 years of dumping raw sewage into the ocean, you finally have a treatment plant.

POOPANOVA
Yes. It's the number 2 story of the day, I would say.

VON ZOOFENDORFEN
Now, well, I think a lot of people will agree with you on that.

POOPANOVA
Yes.

                    VON ZOOFENDORFEN
It must've been a huge
embarrassment for you, over all
these years.

                    POOPANOVA
Well, "sewage" is a rather raw
word. It usually is a hyper-
organic story on social media.

                    VON ZOOFENDORFEN
That it is. So, tell me, what
took so long for this treatment
plant to get up and running?

                    POOPANOVA
Well, you see, bowels of
government move slowly. There
was a system that was working
very well. And it was very
cost-efficient. So, there
wasn't a lot of need for
movement in the bowels of
government on file with a
system that was working well.
So we were cautious to the
point of being paranoid about
any changes.

VON ZOOFENDORFEN
I see. So, what you are saying is that Government was a bit constipated on this issue?

POOPANOVA
Constipated. Cost-effective. Same thing.

VON ZOOFENDORFEN
Well, I mean, it could be said that it was cost-effective because the old system was simply not treating the raw sewage at all. We just dumped it directly into the ocean and the environment basically absorbed the costs and took the lumps on the chin so to speak.

POOPANOVA
Not true. We have been breaking up the lumps for years.

VON ZOOFENDORFEN
And, how were you breaking up the lumps, as you call it? With sticks and shovels?

                    POOPANOVA
          No, no, no. We do this proper
          way, of course! You see, old
          corrugated pipe went way out
          there into deep ocean. Those
          ripply pipes, it's really a
          deliberate design that's like
          the community large intestine.
          It smashes the lumps to bits.

Von Zoofendorfen makes a face like he's
repulsed by the idea.

                 VON ZOOFENDORFEN
          The community's large
          intestine?

                    POOPANOVA
          Yes. It's quite the rough ride
          for floaties, breaking up the
          lumps along the way.

                 VON ZOOFENDORFEN
          This is bordering on too much
          information. Just bordering,
          mind you.

Poopanova is only half-listening.

                    POOPANOVA
          I will miss the efficiency of
          it all. Yeah. So pipe was able
          to shove broken lumps way out
          there into briny ocean which by
          then,

She leans over to whisper like it's some kind
of trade secret.

                    POOPANOVA
          . . . it's just a brown frothy
          slurry mixture that bears no
          resemblance of the feces from
          the human species.

                    VON ZOOFENDORFEN
          I'm sure the creatures in the
          ocean can tell.

                    POOPANOVA
          Maybe. But they don't vote, so
          who cares?

                    VON ZOOFENDORFEN
          All right then. Um. I received
          a report yesterday, and it says
          that there are still very high
          coliform counts and a resident
          recently found, ah, "floaties"
          on a local beach?

                    POOPANOVA
I think the exact term is FECAL
coliform.

                    VON ZOOFENDORFEN
Yuk, that just sounds dirty.

                    POOPANOVA
Well, it is! But see, if there
is such issue, it's not coming
from our region, not possible.
We already know that we broke
up the lumps. So, maybe it's
coming from Fraser River. You
see, Vancouver has been dumping
millions, maybe billions, of
gallons of sewage into Fraser
for years.

                    VON ZOOFENDORFEN
Um. Vancouver's waste is
actually treated before they
dump it into the ocean.

                    POOPANOVA
That's what they tell us. But
maybe they had breach in
system. Maybe they had too much
and did a secret dumpology at
night and it went undetected by
the media and went unreported.
I mean, who really knows how
that got there?

VON ZOOFENDORFEN
Ok, so you think that the floaties on Victoria beaches, ah, made it across the Salish Sea from Vancouver?

POOPANOVA
Of course. Anything is possible. You see, we get all sorts of junk from Japan that floats right across Pacific. So anything is plausible, I mean, possible.

VON ZOOFENDORFEN
Ok, I, I don't think we're getting floaties from Japan.

POOPANOVA
Maybe they are not that good of swimmers, but it is within realm of possibilities that they came from international waters.

She leans in as if to share another secret.

POOPANOVA
You see, I have a great conspiracy theory that this new rash of floaties showing up in our waters is actually from the United States of America.

                    VON ZOOFENDORFEN
          A conspiracy theory?

                    POOPANOVA
          Yes. There is a conspiracy
          theory floating around that
          Americans are trying to enter
          Canada as floaties first and
          the humans follow after.

Poopanova nods knowingly. Von Zoofendorfen
looks bewildered.

                    VON ZOOFENDORFEN
          So are you saying this could be
          an illegal immigration issue?

                    POOPANOVA
          Exactly.

                    VON ZOOFENDORFEN
          That seems preposterous! Why
          would they do that?

                    POOPANOVA
          To avoid detection, of
          course. It's the old smuggling
          trick. You cross the border
          disassembled and reunite the
          pieces on the other side. You
          see, they just slide in quietly
                       (MORE)

POOPANOVA (CONT'D)
on the surface of the water.
Illegal aliens and immigrants
will do anything to get into
a beautiful and great country
like ours.

VON ZOOFENDORFEN
I dunno. I wouldn't want to
reassemble with my floaties.
Maybe it's more like sending
their "floaties" as scouts?

POOPANOVA
Yesss. Good theory! Of course,
it's, it's like test. Think
about it. If they send us
floaties and they arrive on
our shore and no one notices?
Presto. They find a breach in
our security.

VON ZOOFENDORFEN
Ok, ok, that might be a plan,
but we did notice.

POOPANOVA
Yes, but have you seen any of
them cross border yet?

VON ZOOFENDORFEN
Me, myself, personally, no.

POOPANOVA
Exactly. That is my point. They must be slithering into our waters under the darkness of night.

She motions with her hand.

POOPANOVA
Whoosh. They just squirt right across the border and they are in.

Von Zoofendorfen winces at the thought of people squirting.

VON ZOOFENDORFEN
And how do the actual people squirt across the border?

POOPANOVA
Well, they dress up in feces suit and presto, they land on our shores. There is one walking around in Victoria as we speak.

VON ZOOFENDORFEN
Mr. Floatie, I was told, is a local.

POOPANOVA
Local or crazy, same thing, to think we haven't noticed him walking around. But I'm very suspicious that this is the first of the illegal immigrants that have arrived on our shores. That is my point.

VON ZOOFENDORFEN
I'm, I'm sorry. What is your point?

POOPANOVA
Well, my point is, we need to actually beef up our water borders before it is too late. Before these floaties turn into the thousands of people that they belong to.

VON ZOOFENDORFEN
I think you are paranoid.

POOPANOVA
You are not the first to say that, but we let our guard down and wham!

VON ZOOFENDORFEN
What?

POOPANOVA
Yes, next thing you know these large floaties will be blebbing off little bitty floaties along the way. You see, they are reinventing themselves as a brown asexual floatie blebbing organism until they get into Canada, of course.

VON ZOOFENDORFEN
I never thought of feces as possible asexual beings. This sounds more like an alien horror story.

POOPANOVA
It is. Where do you think the term "illegal alien" comes from?

VON ZOOFENDORFEN
Oh, I never thought of that. The next thing you are going to suggest is to build a wall around the country or a dome over it.

POOPANOVA
Geez, those are pretty great ideas you have there.

VON ZOOFENDORFEN
Well, maybe we should bring all this back down to earth. How do you know that this isn't just the United States trying to get even with Canada for all those years of dumping our floaties onto their beaches?

POOPANOVA
Never thought of that either. I think we should strike committee immediately to analyze situation.

VON ZOOFENDORFEN
Ok, so why don't these so-called illegal immigrants just come the usual way, say, maybe, in a car, or train or plane and apply for their visa?

POOPANOVA
Well, they would, except they are most likely draft dodgers and rapists and drug dealers! And they have absolutely no morals. No morals. And I'm sure they don't want us to see their passports.

VON ZOOFENDORFEN
Ok, and how can you tell all of this from floaties?

POOPANOVA
Ah, special Anal Ist data.

VON ZOOFENDORFEN
I'm sorry, did you say Anal Ist? Is that a word or a position?

POOPANOVA
It's both. I think that's how scientists refer to it . . .
(whispering)
Anal Ist data.

VON ZOOFENDORFEN
Oh, ok, well, no matter how well they are positioned or they are poised, what is the Government going to do about it? What actions are you going to take?

POOPANOVA
Ah, very glad you asked this question. You see, I've put forward a private member's bill
(MORE)

POOPANOVA (CONT'D)
in the House to fund super-secretive genetic Anal Ist research on floaties, so we can get to the real bottom of situation.

VON ZOOFENDORFEN
Ok, and what does this super-secretive genetic anal, anal, anala—

POOPANOVA
—Anal Ist—

VON ZOOFENDORFEN
—Anal Ist—

POOPANOVA
—Data—

VON ZOOFENDORFEN
—Anal Ist data of the floaties do?

POOPANOVA
Um, well, this is top secret. I cannot tell you because you are not in the inner bowels of government. But you can trust us.

VON ZOOFENDORFEN
Really? You're going to pull the trust card on me?

POOPANOVA
Ok, I will tell you. This secret Anal Ist data can tell us where potential illegal aliens come from. Like, if they are American or Mexican, for likely example.
        (she whispers)
Or terrorists.

VON ZOOFENDORFEN
Ok, so you really think that by doing anal ist floatie investigations you could uncover a terrorist plot?

POOPANOVA
Of course, in my experience, and I have a lot of experience with terrorist floaties. We can. It's true and it works.

VON ZOOFENDORFEN
Ok, so, how could you tell the floatie's nationality based on genetic anal ist data, as you like to put it?

                    POOPANOVA
That is also top secret. But
I will tell you. It's in the
spices.

                    VON ZOOFENDORFEN
Gross. This is not a fried
chicken recipe, you know.

                    POOPANOVA
It could be.

                    VON ZOOFENDORFEN
Yuck.

                    POOPANOVA
No, that's a separate
investigation that I can't
talk about. It is gross, but
government has to take lead on
gross. We need to protect our
people. It is essential. This
is what we do, Comrade.

                    VON ZOOFENDORFEN
Ok, right. But what if that
does not work?

                    POOPANOVA
Ah, I am also glad you asked
this question, because my
number two approach is this
                    (MORE)

POOPANOVA (CONT'D)
might be an undeclared,
subversive trade issue.

VON ZOOFENDORFEN
An undeclared trade issue?

POOPANOVA
Effectively, I see this
whole issue as a two-pronged
approach.

VON ZOOFENDORFEN
Ew, two prongs? That sounds a
bit rough. I think you just
made many of our viewers'
sphincters tighten right now.

He laughs. Poopanova ignores his concern.

POOPANOVA
I can't help that. This is
serious business.

VON ZOOFENDORFEN
I'm sure it is.

POOPANOVA
No, no, no, no. You see,
Americans are always going on
and on about our cheap logs.
And every time we turn around
(MORE)

POOPANOVA (CONT'D)
they are challenging us under NAFTA or some other bogus agreement, accusing us of, of dumping cheap logs illegally on them.

VON ZOOFENDORFEN
And now, according to you, assuming they are American, you say, they're dumping floatie logs on us.

POOPANOVA
Exactly. They are weaponizing their floaties. Cheap retaliation. You see, we cannot obstruct their floaties without getting accused of interfering in their business. And if we do? Wham! They hit us with export duties. It's all free trade and, and corporate rights, ah, the usual crapola border skirmish things.

VON ZOOFENDORFEN
Ok. Are you thinking we should be slapping some kind of import duty or some kind of tariff on the American floaties as compensation?

> POOPANOVA
>
> Exactly. Tariff is excellent way to show neighbours to the south that two can play log tariff game. And maybe then they will keep their floaties to themselves.

> VON ZOOFENDORFEN
>
> And by that are you also suggesting we send our floaties over the border?

> POOPANOVA
>
> Now you get it, Comrade.

> VON ZOOFENDORFEN
>
> Oh, ok, but Canadians are not trying to sell the American logs at predatory prices. And we are not trying to sell our floaties south of the border. I assume all floaties are usually just made free. So how do we set any value on them, unless, of course, you're considering food as an input cost.

> POOPANOVA
>
> Well, let me explain, Comrade. It is very sneaky, devious American plan that they do very
>
> (MORE)

                    POOPANOVA (CONT'D)
          well. In order to establish
          market share, they introduce
          the products for free. And
          then, when it overtakes
          marketplace, they jack up price
          or sue under free trade to make
          a bunch of money.

She taps her temple.

                    VON ZOOFENDORFEN
          Or they could advertise it like
          it's the next best invention.

                    POOPANOVA
          Exactly!

                    VON ZOOFENDORFEN
          Hmmm. Ok. Sounds like we
          might have to put up with some
          American crap for quite a while
          before this free dumping sorts
          itself out.

                    POOPANOVA
          Maybe, but I have already
          talked with Premier. Very smart
          woman, by the way. And I'm sure
          she will take to top of agenda
          because after all, this is
          about Canadian sovereignty and
                         (MORE)

POOPANOVA (CONT'D)
this issue must be crushed in butt hard before it gets too late.

VON ZOOFENDORFEN
I think you mean nipped in the bud?

POOPANOVA
No, crushed. And crushed hard, Comrade.

VON ZOOFENDORFEN
Ok, wow. That sounds painful.

POOPANOVA
Nothing that is painless is worth doing, Comrade.

VON ZOOFENDORFEN
Ok, well, on that point, a lot of people might agree with you. I, myself, am not one of them. So, would you say this could end up as an anti-trust case in some way?

POOPANOVA
I'm not anti-trust. I think the Americans trust us. I'm quite trustworthy, actually.

                    VON ZOOFENDORFEN
          Well, thank you, and I trust
          that this means that it is the
          end of our interview. Thank you
          so very much, Minister.

                    POOPANOVA
          You're welcome.

Poopanova passes gas. Von Zoofendorfen makes
a face.

                    VON ZOOFENDORFEN
          I'm sorry. Did you say
          something?

                    POOPANOVA
          No, just gas.

                    VON ZOOFENDORFEN
          Very well then.

She passes gas again.

ON VON ZOOFENDORFEN — who is making a face.

                    VON ZOOFENDORFEN
          Well, this has been . . .

Von Zoofendorfen blinks.

                    VON ZOOFENDORFEN
          Oh. Dear lord. Wow, that is.

Poopanova passes more gas and looks down.

>   VON ZOOFENDORFEN
> Good God. I am Francis von
> Zoofendorfen and this has
> been . . .
>   (struggling)
> *Pressure Point.*

                                        FADE TO:

EXT. VANCOUVER SKY (DRONE) — NIGHT

Fireworks, sounding like a fart, explode into the night sky and we . . .

                                        FADE OUT

EPISODE 8:

The Benefits of Surplus Killer Whales

J-C Roy plays Skip Peabrawnee, the Minister of Economic Development, aka the Minister of Surplus Promotions.

                    ANNOUNCER
          Warning. Hyper-sensitive,
          serious and easily offended
          viewers and politicians may
          find that some dialogue will
          make them laugh. Consult your
          physician before consuming this
          content.

AUDIO STATIC, TV COLOUR BARS SPAGHETTI AND
DISAPPEAR

EXT. VANCOUVER CITY (AERIAL) — NIGHT

A brilliant shot of the downtown core all
lit up.

                    VON ZOOFENDORFEN
          It's time for *Pressure Point*.
          Here's what people have been
          watching and hearing in the
          news this week.

AUDIO STATIC, TV COLOUR BARS SPAGHETTI AND
DISAPPEAR

INT. WORKSHOP — AFTERNOON

A TV is perched on a makeshift shelf. It's
showing footage of the Salish Sea. The camera
pans to two killer whales.

                    REPORTER 1
          Several reports have come in
          today regarding the Southern
          Resident Killer Whale
          population. We have a brand new
          baby killer whale swimming with
          L pod.

AUDIO STATIC, TV COLOUR BARS SPAGHETTI AND
DISAPPEAR

INT. BEDROOM — DAY

A TV mounted on the wall is tuned into
another report about the Southern Resident
Killer Whale population.

                    REPORTER 2
          The recent birth of a pair of
          Southern Resident Killer Whales
          has the Government excited that
          the population is recovering.
          Not to waste a sense of renewed
          optimism, officials have just
          announced that the Southern
          Resident Killer Whale no longer
          needs to be protected under the
          Endangered Species Act.

INT. TV ROOM — DAY

Yet another news outlet is reporting on the Southern Resident Killer Whale population.

> REPORTER 3
> One expert lamented that the saddle patch of one youngster looks . . .

The report switches to show a document featuring the lineage of a pod of killer whales.

> REPORTER 3
> . . . suspiciously like that of a Northern Resident Killer Whale, which likely means this new orca is a hybrid offspring of the male known as Big Stud.

AUDIO STATIC, TV COLOUR BARS SPAGHETTI AND DISAPPEAR

INT. TECH BUSINESS — DAY

A TV is mounted next to a phone and is broadcasting a news report from The Green Channel. A Canadian coast guard hovercraft can be seen dragging something.

ZOOMING IN — a diver can be seen jumping into the water on some kind of rescue.

ON A TV MOUNTED ON ANOTHER WALL

The hovercraft is near a whale. Another diver leaps off the side and into the water.

                    REPORTER 4
          Reports came in to various
          government agencies when
          residents around Boundary
          Bay . . .

INT. HOUSE — CONTINUOUS

A tablet leaning against a wall is streaming the news report about the rescue.

                    REPORTER 4
          . . . saw what they thought
          was a killer whale swimming
          upside-down in shallow water.
          Officials located the whale and
          towed it to shore, where they
          announced it was deceased.

INT. OLD KITCHEN — DAY

Someone else is streaming the same report on their cellphone, which is sitting next to the kitchen sink.

                    REPORTER 4
          Forensic veterinarians were
          dispatched to perform a
          necropsy when they saw . . .

INSERT — of footage of a massive boil appears
on screen.

                    REPORTER 4
          . . . a giant boil protruding
          from the whale's side. The
          investigation continues.

AUDIO STATIC, TV COLOUR BARS SPAGHETTI AND
DISAPPEAR

INT. PRINT SHOP — DAY

A radio sits on the counter. It's tuned into
a news report.

                    REPORTER 5
          Another killer whale has
          washed up on shore. It's the
          third death in the endangered
          Southern Resident population
          and it has experts concerned
          that something in the
          environment is killing members
          of this small population.

EXT. AUTO REPAIR SHOP — CONTINUOUS

A mechanic is lying under a car and listening to the news on his ghetto blaster.

>   REPORTER 5
> Several government agencies and scientists are on the scene investigating the whale's death in spite of the fact that these whales are no longer protected under the *Endangered Species Act*.

AUDIO STATIC, TV COLOUR BARS SPAGHETTI AND DISAPPEAR

INT. STEAKHOUSE RESTAURANT — DAY

The wall-mounted TV is tuned into The Green Channel news. A reporter is on a street in Gastown, a district known for collectibles and trinkets.

>   REPORTER 6
> Local business associations are touting a new and emerging industry in limited edition souvenirs and trading cards featuring rare and endangered animals.

TRADING CARDS — featuring several animals fade up on the screen next to the reporter.

                    REPORTER 6
          The more endangered the
          species, the fewer items that
          will be printed or manufactured
          featuring its image. So
          collectors can capitalize on
          not only the rarity of the
          animal,

The trading cards disappear and are replaced with a shot of the rare kermode bear found in the Great Bear Rainforest located on Canada's Pacific coast.

                    REPORTER 6
          . . . but also the rarity of
          the bling associated with it.

INT. OLD BUSINESS OFFICE — CONTINUOUS

The report continues on a desktop computer. The photo of the kermode bear has been replaced by a photo of a human.

                    REPORTER 6
          The move is being hailed
          as a win-win for economic
          development and rare animals in
          our region.

AUDIO STATIC, TV COLOUR BARS SPAGHETTI AND DISAPPEAR

INT. LIVING ROOM — DAY

The TV is tuned into another news channel reporting on recent changes to the status of Canadian oil pipelines. A pipeline under construction is on the screen.

                    REPORTER 2
          On a related note, a private
          member's bill has been put
          forward in the House . . .

BACK TO REPORTER 2 — standing on a beach with Vancouver's downtown as a backdrop.

                    REPORTER 2
          . . . to place pipelines on the
          endangered species list, as
          the number of pipelines in the
          province have been halved from
          two to one.

INT. MODERN RESTAURANT — CONTINUOUS

The pipeline report continues.

                    REPORTER 2
          One expert using tried and true
          statistical calculations has
          estimated that this is close to
          a 50% reduction in the pipeline
          species. Back to you, Al.

AUDIO STATIC, TV COLOUR BARS SPAGHETTI AND
DISAPPEAR

                                       FADE TO:

INTRO ANIMATION

A slick graphic blends images and geometric
shapes, then wraps around to reveal the
title: *Pressure Point*.

AUDIO STATIC, TV COLOUR BARS SPAGHETTI AND
DISAPPEAR

INT. PRESSURE POINT STUDIO — DAY

The host, Francis von Zoofendorfen, looks
into camera.

                    VON ZOOFENDORFEN
          Hello and welcome to *Pressure
          Point*. I'm your host, Francis
          von Zoofendorfen. And joining
          me today is none other than
                      (MORE)

VON ZOOFENDORFEN (CONT'D)
the Minister for Economic Development, Mr. Peabrawnee. Mr. Peabrawnee, hello. And welcome to the show.

PEABRAWNEE
Thanks! Heh, heh.

VON ZOOFENDORFEN
Well, ok, that was not a voice I was expecting. So, tell me, Mr. Peabrawnee, my apologies, but how did you come to be the Minister for Economic Development?

PEABRAWNEE
Well, I haven't got a clue.

VON ZOOFENDORFEN
Why doesn't that surprise me? How shall I call you?

PEABRAWNEE
Whatever you like, as long as it's not late for dinner.

VON ZOOFENDORFEN
Ha! Good one. Ok, then, I'm just going to call you Skip, if that's ok.

                    PEABRAWNEE
          Oh, I like that.

                    VON ZOOFENDORFEN
          Great. Now,

Peabrawnee gives an affirmative grunt.

                    VON ZOOFENDORFEN
          . . . settle down.

                    PEABRAWNEE
          Uh, hmm.

                    VON ZOOFENDORFEN
          All right, well then, Minister
          Skip. This week your ministry,
          as we all heard from the news
          report, announced that Southern
          Resident Killer Whales are no
          longer on the endangered list.

                    PEABRAWNEE
          That's right. This is very good
          news!

                    VON ZOOFENDORFEN
          It is, it's great news. Ah,
          well, I guess it would be great
          news except for the fact that
                         (MORE)

VON ZOOFENDORFEN (CONT'D)
it's a very small population of just 74 killer whales from what I understand.

PEABRAWNEE
Oh, yes. But it's always been that way. The Southern Resident Killer Whales have always been a small population. And they are breeding like rabbits as we speak. We've had six new births this year. And with that many calves, it's no longer appropriate for the Southern Resident Killer Whale to be on the endangered species list.

VON ZOOFENDORFEN
Ok, well, I agree it was a good year but, honestly, we're talking about six new whales, not 60, 600, 6000, 60,000 or even 600,000. We're just talking about one more than five. Six. I would say that this population has a long, long way to go before it's out of danger, don't you think?

                    PEABRAWNEE
          Well, I used to think that!
          But we did a careful analysis.
          And the population is not
          endangered if the reproductive
          rate is this high.

                    VON ZOOFENDORFEN
          And why is that?

                    PEABRAWNEE
          Because you can't be endangered
          if your reproductive rate is,
          well, parabolic.

Peabrawnee makes a motion with his hand like
a parabolic curve.

                    PEABRAWNEE
          So, zip, zip, zip. Not in
          danger.

                    VON ZOOFENDORFEN
          Well, one good year doesn't
          make a trend.

                    PEABRAWNEE
          Oh, right. It's not a trend.
          But who really cares? The
          important thing is, we were
          able to make crucial changes
                    (MORE)

PEABRAWNEE (CONT'D)
in the environment for this species, which we all love, so they could flourish. And look what happened. And thankfully all before the next election, when under a new government, well, heaven forbid, this valuable species might not get the recognition or help it deserves.

VON ZOOFENDORFEN
What do you say to the critics who say that, ah, removing the Southern Resident Killer Whale from the endangered list is nothing more than a stunt to open up the Salish Sea to more oil tankers? And that the endangered designation was just causing a legal headache for the shipment of oil?

Peabrawnee waves his hand in a self-effacing manner.

PEABRAWNEE
Aw, that's not true.

VON ZOOFENDORFEN
It's not?

PEABRAWNEE
We've been fixing a whole pile of laws so it wouldn't matter one way or the other. Heh, heh.

VON ZOOFENDORFEN
Did you say "fixing laws"?

PEABRAWNEE
Yes, just a little jiggling, as governments do.

VON ZOOFENDORFEN
"A little jiggling."

PEABRAWNEE
(nods)
Hmmm.

VON ZOOFENDORFEN
Jiggling?

PEABRAWNEE
Jiggling!

VON ZOOFENDORFEN
Jiggling?

PEABRAWNEE
Yes, jiggling!

VON ZOOFENDORFEN
Not jaggling?

PEABRAWNEE
Nope.

VON ZOOFENDORFEN
Jiggling.

PEABRAWNEE
Jiggling!

VON ZOOFENDORFEN
Jiggling the law.

PEABRAWNEE
Jiggling.

VON ZOOFENDORFEN
A little jiggling of the law so that—

PEABRAWNEE
—Yes. A little jiggle here and a little jiggle there.

Peabrawnee does a little upper-body dance move.

PEABRAWNEE
We often do a little dance to it in the office.

VON ZOOFENDORFEN
I suppose from your government's perspective it's a victory dance of sorts?

Peabrawnee chuckles.

VON ZOOFENDORFEN
Because it wouldn't look good if an oil tanker was to run over an animal that was on an endangered species list. Correct?

PEABRAWNEE
Oh, yes, exactly. That would be terrible.

VON ZOOFENDORFEN
But it's not so bad if your regular out-of-the-box generic species gets its skull crushed by the hull of a ship? That's not so bad?

PEABRAWNEE
Well, politically speaking, yes, not a great scenario either way. But you see, that's the beauty of the six new whales. You see, if one or two die,

Holds up three fingers, oblivious to the error.

                PEABRAWNEE
. . . by my math, we're still up at least four whales. So the oil continues to flow, which means it's getting shipped and we make a bunch of money. Win-win!!

              VON ZOOFENDORFEN
Well, I'm sure the whale that had its head caved in won't see it as a win. But I digress. And I don't think the public will see it as a win-win if there's even one death of a Southern Resident Killer Whale.

                PEABRAWNEE
Ah, but we all die, so it's hardly anything to get really worked up about. And I'm told they are pretty smart and will likely survive.

              VON ZOOFENDORFEN
Likely survive? I think the public needs more assurance that we are protecting an
                  (MORE)

VON ZOOFENDORFEN (CONT'D)
endangered whale population with something more than vague hopes and prayers.

PEABRAWNEE
Basically it all comes down to natural selection. You know, some individuals in a population die quickly, probably before reproducing, because they can't adjust to new circumstances in the environment.

VON ZOOFENDORFEN
Sure, but evolution happens over long periods of time. And the populations have time to adjust. This is obviously different. Humans are changing the environment way too fast.

PEABRAWNEE
Oh well, they'll just have to keep up now, won't they? I think we have the perfect situation here. We have a whole six new whales. All at once. And we can afford to lose a few of the dumb ones that don't know what an oil tanker is.

VON ZOOFENDORFEN
Sorry, did you say "dumb ones"?

PEABRAWNEE
Oh, yes, and with a naturally selected, little smarter Southern Resident population, we get to keep exporting more oil because they know how to get the hell out of the way. Win-win!!

VON ZOOFENDORFEN
I think you are going to have a very difficult time selling the public your government's position on natural selection involving oil tankers.

PEABRAWNEE
Well, we have to modernize these ancient theories of evolution. Right? And presumably, the ones that figure out what an oil tanker is—

VON ZOOFENDORFEN
—Yes, a fast-moving ship with giant propeller blades—

PEABRAWNEE
—would also be better at surviving in the wild. Now, we did consider capturing a few of these once endangered ones, um, so they could live in an aquarium and we could keep them safe and away from the ships.

VON ZOOFENDORFEN
Keep them in an aquarium? Like keeping them in captivity?

PEABRAWNEE
Just for safety reasons, of course. Not like the bad old days of capturing them for entertainment and stuff like that. Just purely for safety reasons.

VON ZOOFENDORFEN
Wow, ok. Safety reasons. Tell me more about this.

PEABRAWNEE
Oh, well, we could even have people go in and see them, and people could even ride them.

VON ZOOFENDORFEN
Wait. What? Ride them?

                    PEABRAWNEE
          And we would have to charge a
          fee, of course, to help with
          the costs of maintaining and
          keeping them. So that we can
          afford to feed them top-of-
          the-line food. I mean, can
          you imagine captive endangered
          killer whales being able to eat
          farmed salmon every day? How
          good is that?!!

                    VON ZOOFENDORFEN
          Well, it sounds like your
          government has all the angles
          figured out on this one.

They both laugh, von Zoofendorfen nervously.

                    PEABRAWNEE
          Well, sort of, I mean. But this
          bonanza of six calves certainly
          changed our overall plan. In
          fact, we're so excited about
          this huge, huge killer whale
          surplus!! Heck, we might even
          sell one or two!!

                    VON ZOOFENDORFEN
          You can't be serious. You're
          thinking of selling one or two?
          Really?

                    PEABRAWNEE
Well, just the really old ones.
You know, before they die and
have no value.

                    VON ZOOFENDORFEN
The old ones.

                    PEABRAWNEE
Oh, yes. We do that all
the time with government
assets . . . sell them off
to our friends, ur, business
partners, to clear out old
inventory and bring in brand
new inventory that is more
maintenance-free. So, in a
way, when we introduce new
challenges to our species of
concern, it's like refreshing
our inventory of animals.

                    VON ZOOFENDORFEN
Well, Skip, I don't think I've
ever heard of anyone referring
to animals in the wild as, ah,
you know, inventory.

                    PEABRAWNEE
It's a really useful way to
look at it. Look at Africa.
Their inventory of some species
                    (MORE)

                    PEABRAWNEE (CONT'D)
          is getting very low. And low
          inventory means that it's
          rare. And, well, the value of
          the rare inventory means that
          it's scarce, and scarcity is a
          really, really good thing. The
          animals on a per unit basis are
          way more valuable.

Peabrawnee makes big swooping motions with
his arms. He's very excited at the thought of
big dollars.

                    VON ZOOFENDORFEN
          Should we really be referring
          to live animals as units? I
          feel like we are talking about
          a company on the stock market,
          not endangered animals.

                    PEABRAWNEE
          Oh, but it's really a terrific
          way to bring clarity to the
          situation, don't you think?

                    VON ZOOFENDORFEN
          Ok. To use your terminology,
          those scarce units would then
          become targets for poachers
          trying to cash in. And that
          could become a very big
          problem.

PEABRAWNEE
Well, yes. It does make the value of the animals more valuable, so that's a problem in one sense.

VON ZOOFENDORFEN
Some would say in every sense.

PEABRAWNEE
Not quite. Think about ivory. Everyone wants ivory, for example, and that rare inventory stimulates excitement. So, from a pure excitement slash, economic slash viewpoint, rare animals stimulate the economy. We took a very big hit by taking this whale species off the endangered list. It reduces the value of one of our natural assets. It was a very big sacrifice on the public ledger that our government made to do the right thing.

VON ZOOFENDORFEN
Ok, that's great. And normally getting animals off the endangered species list is a terrific thing. It means it's
(MORE)

VON ZOOFENDORFEN (CONT'D)
no longer endangered. But in this case, this species is still endangered. Southern Resident Killer Whales are not abundant. Heck, we have more people in a single screening of *Barbie* than the entire population of these whales. Correct?

PEABRAWNEE
Yes. But let's not get all alarmist and freak out about it.

VON ZOOFENDORFEN
Yes, ok. But usually they are taken off the endangered species list because they are no longer endangered. These whales are simply not abundant.

PEABRAWNEE
Correct. I wouldn't say abundant either.

VON ZOOFENDORFEN
Thank you.

PEABRAWNEE
I think we should stick to the word "surplus."

Von Zoofendorfen runs his fingers through his hair, exasperated.

> **VON ZOOFENDORFEN**
> Hmmm.

> **PEABRAWNEE**
> Oh yes, imagine if we, instead, marketed the Southern Residents as rare, we could bring in much more eco-tourism. And that would translate into more economic activity to our region. Another win-win.

> **VON ZOOFENDORFEN**
> Ok.

> **PEABRAWNEE**
> And if they are rare, it might attract poachers, which could be construed as a big negative on the surface. But poachers stay in hotels, buy meals and spend all kinds of money to try and shoot something.

> **VON ZOOFENDORFEN**
> Yikes! Ok.

PEABRAWNEE
And the whales are rare, so these poachers, most of the time, don't shoot anything because they can't find them. So that's another win-win. We get all this money and still have the rare killer whales. I mean, how can we really lose?

VON ZOOFENDORFEN
Yes, but statistically speaking, the longer we allow this, sooner or later the poachers will get lucky and this policy could push these whales to extinction.

PEABRAWNEE
Well, "extinction" is a harsh word. The likelihood of that happening is remote. But let's take that scenario to the logical conclusion.

VON ZOOFENDORFEN
I'm not sure I would be using the word "logical" in any of this. But ok, humour me.

PEABRAWNEE
Well, still not a problem. We could set up museums, gather up some of their bones, um, skeletons, and create an amazing museum that would show their bones and, I dare say, draw millions of tourists to come and see the remaining artifacts of a once great species. Another win-win. You know, kinda like what happens with the dinosaur bones in Alberta. Those museums rake it in. I think we should try and get a bigger share of the tourist-staring-at-dead-stuff economy, don't you think?

VON ZOOFENDORFEN
Tourists staring at dead stuff? Oh my lord.

PEABRAWNEE
Yes, a little preying and a little luck and we could really score big on all of this.

VON ZOOFENDORFEN
Well, there you go. Ah, well, I'm glad we cleared that up!

Von Zoofendorfen looks into camera.

> VON ZOOFENDORFEN
> There you have it, dear viewer. Polished optimism from the grand promoter of the Government, Mr. Skip Peabrawnee, our Minister of Economic Development. The man who, through his wonderful actions, has gotten the Southern Resident Killer Whale off the endangered species list because we now have an abundance of six baby killer whales.

He clears his throat.

> VON ZOOFENDORFEN
> Such optimism.

> PEABRAWNEE
> Optimism is us. Anytime you need a bit of good old promotion, I'm happy to fly a banner about any of our natural resources.

                    VON ZOOFENDORFEN
          Well, thank you, Mr. Peabrawnee,
          for your time. And apparently,
          if you need cheerleading, all
          you have to do is just ring
          up the Minister of Economic
          Development.

                    PEABRAWNEE
          Yay!

                    VON ZOOFENDORFEN
          Thank you, dear viewer, for
          tuning in once again to this
          glorious and wonderful show.
          Mr. Peabrawnee, is there
          anything else you would like to
          say?

Von Zoofendorfen doesn't let Peabrawnee
respond.

                    VON ZOOFENDORFEN
          Oops, well, we are out of time.
          I apologize.

Peabrawnee sits with his mouth hanging open.

                    VON ZOOFENDORFEN
          And to you and to those of
          yours, I say thank you for
          watching. I am your host,
          Francis von Zoofendorfen, and
          this has been . . .
                    (into camera)
          . . . *Pressure Point!*

                                        FADE TO:

EXT. VANCOUVER SKY (DRONE) — NIGHT

Fireworks explode into the night sky and
we . . .

                                        FADE OUT

EPISODE 9:

Climate Change Is a Good Thing

Sarah Marchand plays Sally Dweller, the Prime Minister of Canada, aka the Prime Minister of Beach Economies.

							ANNOUNCER
					Warning. The following program
					contains rude, sassy, adult-
					themed, comical material.
					Hyper-sensitive, serious and
					easily offended viewers and
					politicians may find that some
					dialogue will make them laugh.
					Consult your physician before
					consuming this content.

AUDIO STATIC, TV COLOUR BARS SPAGHETTI AND DISAPPEAR

EXT. VANCOUVER CITY (AERIAL) - NIGHT

A brilliant shot of the downtown core all lit up.

							VON ZOOFENDORFEN
					It's time for *Pressure Point*.
					Here's what people have been
					watching and hearing in the
					news this week.

AUDIO STATIC, TV COLOUR BARS SPAGHETTI AND DISAPPEAR

INT. BAR - NOON

A small TV hanging from the ceiling is tuned into a noon news report. It shows a suburb of Greater Vancouver under a smoky sky.

                    REPORTER 1
          Vancouver has been blanketed
          in smoke for the third week
          in a row as wild fires ravage
          the west coast of the United
          States.

KITSILANO BEACH — the harbour is covered in
smoke.

                    REPORTER 1
          Local officials say that we
          would rather be ravaged . . .

INT. VENDING MACHINE DISTRIBUTOR — CONTINUOUS

A radio on a machine is tuned into the same
news report.

                    REPORTER 1
          . . . right here in British
          Columbia so at least wildfires
          wouldn't become a free trade
          issue and subject to tariffs.

AUDIO STATIC, TV COLOUR BARS SPAGHETTI AND
DISAPPEAR

INT. ARTIST'S STUDIO — LATER

A laptop is streaming a news report about
wildfires in Australia.

                    REPORTER 2
          Heat waves in Australia are
          hitting nearly 50 degrees
          centigrade, literally cooking
          the landscape to a crisp . . .

IMAGE JUMPS — to a massive fire with smoke
billowing into the sky.

                    REPORTER 2
          . . . and feeding wildfires
          that are now being described as
          extreme.

AUDIO STATIC, TV COLOUR BARS SPAGHETTI AND
DISAPPEAR

INT. MECHANIC'S SHOP — DAY

A man is taking a break and watching the news
on his computer.

                    REPORTER 3
          One local politician has said
          that it's extreme to use the
          word "extreme" in extreme news
          reports. He said that even
          using the word "wildfires" is
          inflammatory.

INT. CRAFT SHOP — CONTINUOUS

The staff at this shop is watching the same report.

                    REPORTER 3
     The official stance of all
     levels of government, however,
     is that extreme fires have
     a long way to go before they
     should be considered extreme.
     Stay tuned for a preview of
     next week's breaking news. Back
     to you.

INT. MODERN FURNITURE STORE — DAY

A news report on the wall-mounted TV shows a flash flood ripping through a community.

                    REPORTER 2
     Flash flooding has gripped
     the town of Cache Creek this
     afternoon when six inches of
     rain fell in just a few hours.

INT. BURGER JOINT KITCHEN — MOMENTS LATER

The report blares out of a radio tucked in next to a bun warmer.

                    REPORTER 2
          The wall of water ripped
          through the little community,
          taking cars and buildings with
          it.

INT. LIVING ROOM — CONTINUOUS

A massive shot of farms underwater.

                    REPORTER 2
          One optimistic official said
          that at least the local crops
          got a good watering,

INT. BURGER JOINT — CONTINUOUS

The same report blasts out of the radio on the counter.

                    REPORTER 2
          . . . even though half of them
          were covered in mud.

AUDIO STATIC, TV COLOUR BARS SPAGHETTI AND DISAPPEAR

INT. GREENHOUSE — DAY

A cellphone is streaming a news report about the smoky skies.

                    REPORTER 4
          In a recent press conference,
          Canadian officials have
          indicated that they will be
          favouring domestically produced
          respiratory hazards over
          American smoke imports.

INT. PIZZA PARLOUR KITCHEN — CONTINUOUS

The staff TV hangs on the wall.

                    REPORTER 4
          The officials fear that the
          American smoke pouring over the
          border could lead to a trade
          dispute and trigger a tit-for-
          tat escalation in tariffs on
          carcinogenic inhalants.

INT. BAR — MOMENTS LATER

The report is being watched by bar patrons across town.

                    REPORTER 4
          An expert who spoke to us on
          condition of anonymity told
          us that the big tech offering
          of free goods is merely a ploy
          and . . .

ON ENGLISH BAY — the sky is very dark with smoke and the orange sun reflecting off the water looks apocalyptic.

> REPORTER 4
> . . . once they have cornered the market on post-apocalyptic haze, they will be raising prices on suffocating Canadians.

AUDIO STATIC, TV COLOUR BARS SPAGHETTI AND DISAPPEAR

INTRO ANIMATION

A slick graphic blends images and geometric shapes, then wraps around to reveal the title: *Pressure Point*.

AUDIO STATIC, TV COLOUR BARS SPAGHETTI AND DISAPPEAR

INT. PRESSURE POINT STUDIO — DAY

The host, Francis von Zoofendorfen, looks into camera.

> VON ZOOFENDORFEN
> Hello and welcome to *Pressure Point*. I'm your host, Francis von Zoofendorfen. And joining
> (MORE)

                    VON ZOOFENDORFEN (CONT'D)
               me today is a very special
               guest that we've been trying to
               get for many, many months.

WIDER — to reveal the guest.

                    VON ZOOFENDORFEN
               Today's guest is none other
               than our prime minister, Sally
               Dweller. Welcome to the show,
               Ms. Dweller.

DWELLER — with lipstick on her teeth and a
Bronx accent.

                    DWELLER
               Oh, I'm so glad to be here.

                    VON ZOOFENDORFEN
               So, Madam Prime Minister,
               we've had quite the year of
               disasters around the globe
               from wildfires, storms, floods
               and droughts. Even asphalt has
               liquefied in 50-plus degree
               heat in India.

                    DWELLER
               Yes, yes, it's all been a very
               terrible time for sure, hasn't
                         (MORE)

DWELLER (CONT'D)
it? I'm very glad to be chatting with you about this today.

VON ZOOFENDORFEN
And I'm glad that you are glad and we are very glad that you are glad.

DWELLER
We're all glad.

VON ZOOFENDORFEN
So glad.

DWELLER
Yes, I'm glad.

VON ZOOFENDORFEN
Now, clearly the public, if it wasn't concerned before these last few years, it surely is now. The disasters around the globe just keep piling up. That is a fact.

DWELLER
Yes, that is a fact, but so is the fact that with our Earth, there is always the chance
(MORE)

DWELLER (CONT'D)
the sun will heat up a flat surface. I mean, we are just like a great big flat pane of glass floating along in space, and when the angle is just right, it will get hot.

VON ZOOFENDORFEN
Yes, global warming is definitely a pain in the glass, as you say. But—

DWELLER
—But this means that the warming of our planet has everything to do with trigonometry and hardly anything we puny little humans are doing in the giant cosmos of the universe.

VON ZOOFENDORFEN
Well, I didn't realize I had a flat Earther here in front of me. My goodness, some of my best friends are flat Earthers.

Von Zoofendorfen looks into camera.

                    VON ZOOFENDORFEN
          Don't be offended, my flat
          Earther buddies. This
          conversation is to stimulate a
          little debate with our esteemed
          prime minister.

He looks back at Dweller.

                    VON ZOOFENDORFEN
          Now, you can't deny humans
          are burning a lot of fossil
          fuels and that does put a lot
          of carbon out our collective
          tailpipes and into the
          atmosphere.

                    DWELLER
          Yes, yes. But I have been given
          some very detailed research
          that every couple of hundred
          years our flat plate of a
          planet hits the perfect angle
          to the sun and presto, it gets
          a little warmer. No big deal.
          It's all just a wonderful part
          of nature.

                    VON ZOOFENDORFEN
          So you don't place any blame
          whatsoever on our use of fossil
          fuels for this alarming rise in
          global temperatures?

                    DWELLER
          Well, perhaps a smidgen.

She puts up her hand and pinches an imaginary bit of something between her finger and thumb.

                    DWELLER
          But I'm of the opinion that
          the media really tends to
          overdo it, ya know? They
          sensationalize every little
          thing these days. Everything is
          a great big headline like it's
          an earth-shattering event. My
          gosh, we all must know by now
          that it's what makes the media
          sector tick. So, my hat's off
          to them for doing what they do
          well for their shareholders.
          But that's not my opinion at
          all.

                    VON ZOOFENDORFEN
          Oh, ok, so you're saying that
          climate change is nothing but a
          bunch of hype?

                    DWELLER
          Well, it sells a bunch of
          papers, doesn't it?

VON ZOOFENDORFEN
Ok, I suppose it would if people still bought newspapers and read them. But there appears to be overwhelming evidence that climate change and global warming are not only escalating, but we are close to a point of no return. And from all the research that we have ascertained for this show, humans are primarily to blame, not trigonometry.

DWELLER
Look, I like to read. And I'm of the opinion that the whole global warming, climate change thing is way overblown, if you know what I mean.

VON ZOOFENDORFEN
Well, I have right here in my notes the results of a global survey that show that 10,000 climate scientists from across this planet have all come to a consensus that climate change is real.

Dweller scoffs and giggles.

                    DWELLER
          Hah. Fake. I don't believe
          that.

                    VON ZOOFENDORFEN
          Fake? You don't believe that
          10,000 scientists have come to
          a consensus about it? Or—

                    DWELLER
          —Ten thousand? It has to be
          fake, I mean, really, I doubt
          that there are even 10,000
          scientists. That number seems
          very large to me. It must be
          made up. There aren't that many
          smart people on planet Earth.

                    VON ZOOFENDORFEN
          Ok, I'm gonna just, and please
          don't be offended by this in
          anyway whatsoever, this is
          not me paternalizing in any
          way. But there are 7.5 billion
          people on the planet. Maybe
          more, maybe less. But that's
          a lot of people and there are
          millions that have spent years
          at university. So, I think it's
          safe to say, we have at least
          10,000 intelligent scientists
          on the planet.

                    DWELLER
Seven point five billion people
seems like a very large number
to me. But I've been proven
wrong before. The only time
I've heard numbers like that is
when we look at the budget. I'm
still of the opinion that this
is just a lot of hype.

                    VON ZOOFENDORFEN
A lot of hype.

                    DWELLER
Yeah.

                    VON ZOOFENDORFEN
Ok, well, what about the
numbers like carbon dioxide is
now over 400 parts per million
in the atmosphere?

                    DWELLER
I would outright dispute that.

                    VON ZOOFENDORFEN
And how would you dispute that?

                    DWELLER
Well, look, I agree there's a
lot of numbers, he said, she
said, they said, being thrown
                    (MORE)

> DWELLER (CONT'D)
> around all over the place. I think it's just a bunch of narcissistic people who want to sound important. What I think you need to do is look into who sponsored that research. I'll betcha ten dollars it was some left-leaning woke think tank.

> VON ZOOFENDORFEN
> Woke think tank.

> DWELLER
> Yeah, ah hah, ah hah and there's that old saying, you young children might not be familiar with it. But it goes like this: There are facts and then there are non-facts.

> VON ZOOFENDORFEN
> Whoop. You mean statistics.

> DWELLER
> No, no, no, no, no. Statistics are not facts. Facts are facts plain and simple.

VON ZOOFENDORFEN
Well, not to sound rude or anything, but plain and simple does sound, well, plain and simple.

DWELLER
That's because it is! Look, you can pretty much take the same data and give it to two scientists and they will likely come to totally different conclusions.

VON ZOOFENDORFEN
So, just so I'm clear on this, you don't believe that any peer-reviewed numbers are real?

DWELLER
Peer. Smear. No. No. It seems to me that you are just getting sucked into a whole pile of fake news.

VON ZOOFENDORFEN
Do you believe in any science at all?

                    DWELLER
          Look, science is generally
          not good when it comes to the
          economy. It gets in the way
          of real decision-making and
          it creates uncertainty, and
          uncertainty is bad for business
          and the economy. So, yes, we're
          trying to get that fake news
          out of the government and
          firing the whole pile of them.
          I believe we should just act by
          gut instinct and wilful bliss.

                    VON ZOOFENDORFEN
          Wilful bliss. Wow. Ok, so, you
          want to fire them. So you don't
          want to just muzzle them?

                    DWELLER
          No, no, no, no, no, no. They
          aren't dogs. But come to think
          about it, muzzling them would
          mean they can't talk to the
          media, so that could be a
          better strategy than cutting a
          loose cannon loose, if you know
          what I mean. Ha! But I should
          use my inside voice for that
          idea.

She chuckles at the thought.

VON ZOOFENDORFEN
You probably should. Why don't we switch it up? What about your government's decision to stay out of the Paris talks?

DWELLER
Ah, Paris. Oui, oui!

VON ZOOFENDORFEN
Oui!

DWELLER
Hah. Do you know other countries want us to stop selling our resources and that's preposterous and not negotiable?

VON ZOOFENDORFEN
You mean our oil and gas.

DWELLER
Precisely. I mean, how are we supposed to pay for health care and education?

VON ZOOFENDORFEN
That seems to be the go-to line for every politician when they want to do something that might be perceived as unpopular.

DWELLER
Well, it's true. Health care and education cost more than a bag of potato chips.

VON ZOOFENDORFEN
I'm sure they do, but higher carbon dioxide and pollution in general is adding to human health problems. So aren't we just in a giant downward spiral?

DWELLER
Absolutely. But you don't understand. That's a really, really good thing for the economy to be in a downward spiral with poor health on an individual basis leading the way. If those poor health numbers move the needle at a population level, that's fantastic news for the average everyday healthcare worker!

VON ZOOFENDORFEN
Yes, because that means we are selling more oil and gas, right?

DWELLER
No, no, no. Never mind what caused them to be sick. On their own, people getting sick is good for the economy.

VON ZOOFENDORFEN
People getting sick from poor air quality is a good thing?

DWELLER
Yes! It's wonderful on two fronts. First of all, if we have pollution, that means we have a good economy. And poor air quality means that the healthcare sector is doing very well. Lots of good customers seeking healthcare services. Lots of job opportunities! Nothing wrong with that, is there?

VON ZOOFENDORFEN
Well, I mean, on the surface, perhaps. But if you go to its logical conclusion, what if the temperature of the globe gets so hot that people simply can't work? I mean, how does that fit into your good economy scenario?

                    DWELLER
          Oh, that's even better. There
          will be more activity in the
          tourist sector, lots of people
          going to the beach . . . You
          like going to the beach, don't
          you?

                    VON ZOOFENDORFEN
          I love it.

                    DWELLER
          Me too!

ON DWELLER

                    DWELLER
          Well, that's even better. There
          will be more activity with
          people going to the beach,
          people working on the beach,
          playing on the beach, sleeping
          in tents on the beach. Ah-huh.
          And just think of all the goods
          and services they will need
          like hot dogs, beach blankets,
          mustard, ketchup, pop, cups,
          towels. I mean, the list is
          endless. This is all very, very
          good news.

BACK TO VON ZOOFENDORFEN

                    VON ZOOFENDORFEN
          Ok, but we've already seen
          what all these extreme climate
          events like droughts, and
          fires, and floods destroying
          crops are doing to the economy.
          It looks like a great big
          negative. It's a mess.

INTERCUT — between them.

                    DWELLER
          Heh, heh, heh. One step ahead
          of ya.

                    VON ZOOFENDORFEN
          Good!

                    DWELLER
          Listen.

                    VON ZOOFENDORFEN
          I will.

                    DWELLER
          Look at all the renovations
          that companies will have to do
          to deal with hotter and drier
          conditions, look at all the
          equipment that will need to be
          replaced. And I'm sure some
                         (MORE)

DWELLER (CONT'D)
enterprising folks will use the lack of water to turn out more beef jerky, for example.

VON ZOOFENDORFEN
Beef jerky is your answer to climate change?

DWELLER
Well, it's a start, isn't it?

VON ZOOFENDORFEN
"Start" isn't the word that came to me.

DWELLER
Ok, look, they could also buy shares in food production and distribution companies. Look. Prices of scarce products will go up, and so if food prices escalate, so will the profits. Canada is a commodity-based economy, so that will increase our exports and help us balance out the budget.

VON ZOOFENDORFEN
Ok, but what if the food prices get so high because crops are so rare that the common people simply cannot afford food?

DWELLER
Ah-huh. No problem at all. We will just send them more money on their welfare cheques.

VON ZOOFENDORFEN
Ok, but wouldn't that then just increase public debt?

DWELLER
Heh! Heh! Heh! Heh! No offence, but I can clearly see that you don't read.

VON ZOOFENDORFEN
No offence taken.

DWELLER
Heh, heh, heh. No one cares about public debt because it's not real. Look, the only real debt is corporate debt.

VON ZOOFENDORFEN
Ok, well, let's just continue with this journey. Let's also take this one to its dire conclusion. What if people start dying?

                    DWELLER
          Ok, come on now, let's not get
          crazy here. Obviously, we don't
          want that to happen. But, all
          right, fine. I will humour you.
          Heh! Heh!

                    VON ZOOFENDORFEN
          I'm beginning to wonder about
          that.

                    DWELLER
          Wonder no more.

ON DWELLER

                    VON ZOOFENDORFEN (O.S.)
          Ok.

                    DWELLER
          We've got our own little study
          on how to keep people alive
          during natural disasters so
          we don't lose the innate
          consumption of goods and
          services built into every human
          being. You and I both know that
          extending human life is crucial
          to the economy. I mean, that's
          the only real reason for health
                         (MORE)

DWELLER (CONT'D)
care at all. Why, why do you think politicians care so much about health care?

VON ZOOFENDORFEN
Because if people die it would lead to a loss in consumerism?

DWELLER
Ah, yes, yes, now you get it! We don't want good customers to start dying all over the place. That would be very, very, very, very bad news as opposed to fake news we talked about earlier. Actually, now that I think of it, funeral homes would do quite well, I suspect.

VON ZOOFENDORFEN
Yeah, I imagine they would, sure.

DWELLER
Yeah, I'm glad we figured that out.

VON ZOOFENDORFEN
Ok.

                    DWELLER
          You know, I told the Finance
          Minister that interviews are
          not all bad. This is a perfect
          example of why. Don't you
          think? We discovered something
          important here.

                    VON ZOOFENDORFEN
          We did?

                    DWELLER
          Yes. Actually, I think I'd
          better call my broker and add
          some exposure to funeral homes.

She picks up her phone and begins to dial.

                    VON ZOOFENDORFEN
          Well, you could wait until
          after . . .

BACK TO VON ZOOFENDORFEN

                    VON ZOOFENDORFEN
          Ok. All right, sounds like
          you have it all covered, Prime
          Minister.

                    DWELLER
          You can never be too prepared.
          I really hope to retire soon.

                    VON ZOOFENDORFEN
What about your five-star
pension?

                    DWELLER
Well, it's not as much as you
think.

                    VON ZOOFENDORFEN
Ok, that's something that we
just learned. Well, ah, so just
in summation, your best advice,
Madam Prime Minister, is to buy
shares in sectors that do well
during disasters and then cross
your fingers and hope that it
will all work out in the end?

                    DWELLER
Yeah. And pray.

                    VON ZOOFENDORFEN
Absolutely. That's essential
to all disasters, thoughts and
prayers. Well, Prime Minister,
thank you very much for your
time.

She doesn't respond. She's on her phone and
plugging her other ear to block out von
Zoofendorfen.

                    DWELLER
          Hi, Penny. Can you recommend a
          good funeral home stock?

                    VON ZOOFENDORFEN (O.S.)
          I can see you're busy.

ON VON ZOOFENDORFEN

                    VON ZOOFENDORFEN
          So I'm going to wrap this up if
          that's not too much trouble for
          you. Ok. She's on the phone.
          Well, that seems to be all the
          time we have today, ladies and
          gentlemen.

He glances over at Dweller, who is still
chatting on the phone. Then back to camera.

                    VON ZOOFENDORFEN
          I would like to thank the Prime
          Minister for being here. For
          her enlightening us about her
          ideas and perceptions of global
          warming. Or as the kids these
          days call it, climate change.
          Until next time, I'm your host,
          Francis von Zoofendorfen. And
          this has been *Pressure Point*.

                                        FADE TO:

EXT. VANCOUVER SKY (DRONE) — NIGHT

Fireworks explode into the night sky and we go to . . .

FADE OUT

EPISODE 10:

Evasive Techniques 101

Requell Jodeah plays Candy Barkson, the Premier of British Columbia, aka the Premier of Job-Related Court Proceedings.

                    ANNOUNCER
          Warning. Hyper-sensitive,
          serious and easily offended
          viewers and politicians may
          find that some dialogue will
          make them laugh. Consult your
          physician before consuming this
          content.

AUDIO STATIC, TV COLOUR BARS SPAGHETTI AND
DISAPPEAR

EXT. VANCOUVER CITY (AERIAL) - NIGHT

A brilliant shot of the downtown core all
lit up.

                    VON ZOOFENDORFEN
          It's time for *Pressure Point*.
          Here's what people have been
          watching and hearing in the
          news this week.

AUDIO STATIC, TV COLOUR BARS SPAGHETTI AND
DISAPPEAR

INT. VAN - DAY

It's a bright, sunny day. The radio is tuned
into a news report about the latest on the
Site C dam project in Northern BC.

                    REPORTER 1
          A press conference today to
          update the public on the
          troubled Site C dam project
          revealed massive overruns in
          costs. Officials say that the
          problems started under the
          right bank,

INT. NURSING HOME — CONTINUOUS

A woman is watching the same story on her iPad. A fracking operation is seen from the air.

                    REPORTER 1
          . . . where apparently fracking
          in the area has destabilized
          the valley.

AUDIO STATIC, TV COLOUR BARS SPAGHETTI AND DISAPPEAR

INT. HOME GARAGE SHOP — DAY

The TV on the bench is tuned to The Green Channel news. A reporter is standing outside the Court of Appeal.

> REPORTER 2
> Press conferences have become so routine in our fair city that even the journalists have become numb to the meaningless non-answers given at this time of crisis.

AUDIO STATIC, TV COLOUR BARS SPAGHETTI AND DISAPPEAR

INT. ACCOUNTANT'S OFFICE — DAY

A cute clock radio sits among the usual accountancy paraphernalia.

> REPORTER 1
> I'm here attending yet another press conference where there are few details and even fewer facts being shared with the public.

AUDIO STATIC, TV COLOUR BARS SPAGHETTI AND DISAPPEAR

INT. DINING NOOK — DAY

A subscriber to the *Spoiled Thoughts* newspaper is reading aloud an article about the Site C dam.

                    NEWSPAPER SUBSCRIBER
                "The Province decided that it
                must proceed . . .

PUSHING IN — on the headline which reads
"Site C makes No Cents."

                    NEWSPAPER SUBSCRIBER
                . . . with the Site C project."

AUDIO STATIC, TV COLOUR BARS SPAGHETTI AND
DISAPPEAR

INT. EMPTY OFFICE — LATER

A clock radio is on, but it looks like the
office is empty.

                    REPORTER 1
                The Site C dam is a massive
                construction project that is
                many years away, but this has
                not stopped demonstrators from
                voicing their concerns over
                the . . .

INT. PRINT SHOP — CONTINUOUS

The office TV is tuned to the news report. We
see a tractor hauling a load across a field.

                    REPORTER 1
          . . . impact on farmland, First
          Nations rights, wildlife
          and . . .

INT. FAST LUBE SHOP — CONTINUOUS

A beat-up radio soldiers on, carrying the
news to the customers.

                    REPORTER 1
          . . . even the sacred burial
          grounds of the Peace River
          Valley.

AUDIO STATIC, TV COLOUR BARS SPAGHETTI AND
DISAPPEAR

Yet another radio, this one on a cluttered
shelf in a distribution company warehouse.

                    REPORTER 1
          Government officials say
          there is no irony in giving
          permits to a non-green energy
          project . . .

INT. DINING ROOM — CONTINUOUS

A small TV is sitting on a sideboard. The
image on the screen is a massive fracking
operation near Site C.

                    REPORTER 1
           . . . in the area that adds
           to the cost of a green energy
           project.

INT. CHINESE RESTAURANT — CONTINUOUS

The TV is wall-mounted so customers can see
the news. A series of settling ponds can be
seen next to the main operation.

                    REPORTER 1
           When asked if there would
           ultimately be a net benefit to
           the public,

A SPINNING NEWSPAPER — the *Northern Comment*,
headline reads "No Comment!"

                    REPORTER 1
           . . . the panel unanimously
           said, "No comment."

AUDIO STATIC, TV COLOUR BARS SPAGHETTI AND
DISAPPEAR

INTRO ANIMATION

A slick graphic blends images and geometric
shapes, then wraps around to reveal the
title: *Pressure Point*.

AUDIO STATIC, TV COLOUR BARS SPAGHETTI AND DISAPPEAR

INT. PRESSURE POINT STUDIO — DAY

The host, Francis von Zoofendorfen, looks into camera.

> VON ZOOFENDORFEN
> Hello and welcome to *Pressure Point*. I'm your host, Francis von Zoofendorfen. Joining me today is none other than the premier of our province, Ms. Candy Barkson. Madam Premier, welcome to the show.

> BARKSON
> Thank you. I'm so pleased to be here.

> VON ZOOFENDORFEN
> Well, we are so pleased to have you here. I guess one could say you are today's premier guest.

> BARKSON
> Ha! Ha! Ha! Ha! Ha!

They both laugh.

> BARKSON
> Thank you.

VON ZOOFENDORFEN
No, thank *you*! Let's get down to business, shall we?

BARKSON
Aye.

VON ZOOFENDORFEN
Now, as everyone knows, you've officially broken ground on the Site C dam. A dam that many thought would not be built.

BARKSON
I'm so thrilled to be breaking ground.

VON ZOOFENDORFEN
Well, like they also say, it is better to break ground than it is to break wind.

Barkson wrinkles her nose and chuckles awkwardly.

VON ZOOFENDORFEN
Now, it has also been reported by other news outlets that construction of the dam has been underway for a couple of years. Correct?

BARKSON
Yes, we've been doing a little test digging.

VON ZOOFENDORFEN
Test digging. Looks like from the millions of tons of dirt that have been moved you're doing a lot of test digging.

BARKSON
Correct.

VON ZOOFENDORFEN
But none of this test digging has gone through any kind of formal approval process, has it?

BARKSON
Aye. You just don't know about it.

VON ZOOFENDORFEN
What? Ok, first of all, why doesn't the public know about it? And second, isn't it highly inappropriate for such a massive project to be going ahead when all of the decision-making is behind locked and closed doors?

BARKSON
Well, the Government's doors are not locked per se, they just aren't open to random people. Besides, I can't answer that because it's before the courts.

VON ZOOFENDORFEN
Before the courts? What's before the courts?

BARKSON
The lawsuit.

VON ZOOFENDORFEN
What lawsuit?

BARKSON
Um, the one that's before the courts.

VON ZOOFENDORFEN
What's the nature of the claim?

BARKSON
It's the usual run-of-the-mill, very routine lawsuit. Par for the course, as they say, when it comes to big projects.

VON ZOOFENDORFEN
I see. So, you can't talk about the dam construction because it's before the courts. Right?

BARKSON
That's right, yes.

VON ZOOFENDORFEN
Can you at least tell us which courts?

BARKSON
No. Eh, it's not exactly before the courts. But we always anticipate that it will be before the courts at some point. So we don't talk about it.

VON ZOOFENDORFEN
Ok, so, is it your government's policy to not talk about projects or issues that are before the courts?

BARKSON
That's right. Ya.

VON ZOOFENDORFEN
Ok, and issues that at some time in the future could be before the courts?

BARKSON
That's absolutely right, ya.

VON ZOOFENDORFEN
Ok, well, what can you talk about?

BARKSON
Nothin' of substance, really. But I can talk about jobs.

VON ZOOFENDORFEN
So you can talk about the dam jobs!

BARKSON
Ah, ya, don't hafta 'cus . . . Aye, we can talk about real jobs.

VON ZOOFENDORFEN
Ok, so how many jobs at Site C have you created?

BARKSON
Well, officially, none. Test digging doesn't qualify as real jobs. It's just test digging.

VON ZOOFENDORFEN
I see. So, tell me, what about real jobs?

BARKSON
Well, we are the number one province in the country for creating new real sustainable jobs.

VON ZOOFENDORFEN
Ok, that's great. So, can we talk about the new liquid natural gas plant that has been green-lit?

BARKSON
I cannot talk about the LNG.

VON ZOOFENDORFEN
And why not?

Then in unison.

VON ZOOFENDORFEN AND BARKSON
It's before the courts.

VON ZOOFENDORFEN
Why is it before the courts?

BARKSON
Well, it's not exactly before the courts, you know, but it will be. And out of a preponderance of caution—

VON ZOOFENDORFEN
—You can't say a thing?

BARKSON
Right.

Barkson shakes her head.

VON ZOOFENDORFEN
Oh, and I presume that it doesn't matter what court it would be before.

BARKSON
No.

VON ZOOFENDORFEN
Not even if it's before, let's say, a food court or even a tennis court.

BARKSON
(chuckles)
Not even then.

VON ZOOFENDORFEN
I see. So you can't talk about the environmental implications of the LNG project?

BARKSON
Not even a bit.

                    VON ZOOFENDORFEN
All right. So, what about this?
Can you talk about the jobs
that have been created?

                    BARKSON
Yes, I can absolutely talk
about the real jobs.

                    VON ZOOFENDORFEN
Ok, so how many real, permanent
jobs will there be once the LNG
plant is built?

                    BARKSON
There will be exactly 18,126
construction jobs.

                    VON ZOOFENDORFEN
Wow!

                    BARKSON
I know. Impressive, right?!

                    VON ZOOFENDORFEN
Yes, but those are temporary
jobs. They end once
construction is finished. What
about the permanent jobs?

BARKSON

Well, it takes a very long time to build these projects. So it could be many, many years before these projects are completed. And certainly longer than my term in office. So, as far as I'm concerned, those are real, permanent jobs.

VON ZOOFENDORFEN

Ok, so how many real permanent jobs will last after the construction phase? In other words, how many jobs will there be to operate the LNG plant after construction?

BARKSON

That's way too early to tell. And beyond my scope of office, really.

VON ZOOFENDORFEN

Too early to tell?

BARKSON

Yes.

VON ZOOFENDORFEN
I've been told these new facilities are so automated that there will be three permanent jobs likely outsourced to India or some other country where they'll just push buttons for very low wages.

BARKSON
That's before the courts.

VON ZOOFENDORFEN
What? The number of jobs is before the courts?

BARKSON
Precisely.

VON ZOOFENDORFEN
Canadian jobs?

BARKSON
I cannot comment on that.

VON ZOOFENDORFEN
Ok, Madam Premier, let's try this. In summary, Site C is before the courts. LNG is before the courts. It seems that all of your job creation projects are before the courts.

BARKSON
I cannot comment on that either.

VON ZOOFENDORFEN
Ok, well, since we are on the job bandwagon, how are the negotiations going with the teachers?

He chuckles.

BARKSON
(sighs)
Oh, the teachers! What can I say about the teachers?

VON ZOOFENDORFEN
They say you're trying to cut jobs.

BARKSON
Those are not real full-time jobs, just hypothetical full-time jobs. They are part-time at best. I mean, teachers barely work, like four hours a day. And the union goes on and on and on about the why fors, the whatevers and the whatnots. It's all rather tedious over
(MORE)

BARKSON (CONT'D)
silly part-time work. Taxpayer-funded part-time work, I might add. These are not real jobs. Only private sector jobs are real jobs.

VON ZOOFENDORFEN
It seems we've struck on a bit of a sore point with your government's job creation record.

Barkson glowers at him.

VON ZOOFENDORFEN
So, effectively, you are saying that the jobs created for infrastructure like dams or roads, which are funded by the taxpayer but provided through private companies, are somehow more desirable than teaching jobs that are paid directly by the government. Is that what you are saying?

BARKSON
That's right.

VON ZOOFENDORFEN
How is that better?

BARKSON
It's better because we, the public, we don't get saddled with gold-plated pensions that are a noose around our collective necks. That's how it's better.

VON ZOOFENDORFEN
So are all pensions with the public service a noose, as you call it? Like MLA pensions, for example?

BARKSON
That's different.

VON ZOOFENDORFEN
How so? Sorry. I'm having trouble following your logic.

BARKSON
I can barely follow my own logic, that's why I'm the premier. It's not important to be logical. It's important to lead through foggy, troubled times.

VON ZOOFENDORFEN
Well, I can agree with the fogginess of all of this. I'm glad to hear we are in good hands.

BARKSON
You are! Trust me, you have the best in leadership.

VON ZOOFENDORFEN
So, let me ask you this. Are you anticipating a court challenge with the job cuts affecting the teachers?

BARKSON
Correct. I shoulda mentioned it earlier, but, um, I cannot talk about anything that is, might be or could be before the courts, especially involving the teachers.

VON ZOOFENDORFEN
Ok, that's one thing you've been clear on. How about this? The pipeline. Are you in favour of it?

BARKSON
I'm consulting my team on that.

VON ZOOFENDORFEN
On whether or not you are in favour of it?

BARKSON
Correct.

VON ZOOFENDORFEN
Correct?

BARKSON
Correct.

VON ZOOFENDORFEN
Correct?

BARKSON
Correct.

VON ZOOFENDORFEN
Correct?

BARKSON
Correct.

VON ZOOFENDORFEN
Yes?

BARKSON
Yes.

VON ZOOFENDORFEN
You are saying "yes"?

BARKSON
Yes.

VON ZOOFENDORFEN
Absolutely?

BARKSON
Absolutely.

VON ZOOFENDORFEN
Positively?

BARKSON
Positively.

VON ZOOFENDORFEN
Without any doubt?

BARKSON
Without any doubt.

VON ZOOFENDORFEN
Correctomundo?

BARKSON
Correctomundo. Yes.

VON ZOOFENDORFEN
Absolutely.

BARKSON
Absolutely.

VON ZOOFENDORFEN
Yes.

BARKSON
Yes.

VON ZOOFENDORFEN
Yes.

BARKSON
Yes.

VON ZOOFENDORFEN
Yeeeessss.

BARKSON
Yesss. Aye.

VON ZOOFENDORFEN
Yeessss.

BARKSON
Yessss.

VON ZOOFENDORFEN
No doubt?

BARKSON
No doubt!

VON ZOOFENDORFEN
You don't have a personal viewpoint on the matter?

BARKSON
Correct. It's not the premier's job to have a viewpoint. I'm only supposed to lead the team. And the team hasn't told me yet what my opinion is.

VON ZOOFENDORFEN
So you need to be told what your opinion is on whether or not the pipeline should be built?

BARKSON
Correct.

Von Zoofendorfen sighs.

VON ZOOFENDORFEN
Would you say that your lack of position on this or any other project might have to do with the fact that the election is just a few months away?

BARKSON
Not at all. I'll have you know, I haven't had a strong opinion since I took office.

VON ZOOFENDORFEN
No?

BARKSON
No.

VON ZOOFENDORFEN
None?

BARKSON
None.

VON ZOOFENDORFEN
Zero?

BARKSON
Zero.

VON ZOOFENDORFEN
Zilch?

BARKSON
Zilch.

VON ZOOFENDORFEN
Nada?

BARKSON
Nada.

VON ZOOFENDORFEN
Nothing?

BARKSON
Nothing.

VON ZOOFENDORFEN
Not a one?

BARKSON
Not a one.

VON ZOOFENDORFEN
None whatsoever?

BARKSON
None whatsoever.

VON ZOOFENDORFEN
Zero?

BARKSON
Zero.

VON ZOOFENDORFEN
And why is that?

BARKSON
Well, I haven't had a strong reason to have one. The public doesn't expect one, and I'm a firm believer in giving the public what it wants.

VON ZOOFENDORFEN
Isn't that a bit wishy-washy?

BARKSON
Wishy-washy? I'm not wishy-washy about this at all. I give the public what it wants, nothing of substance.

VON ZOOFENDORFEN
So, is this a self-made method you've developed from experience, or is this a political science theory from some textbook?

BARKSON
Oh, I rarely read, so it didn't come from something like that.

VON ZOOFENDORFEN
You don't read.

BARKSON
Nope. I have people for that. Listen, Joe and Jane Public don't want to know all about the bad things governments have to deal with. That's why they elect a few people to do all the dirty work.

VON ZOOFENDORFEN
Well, if I may, Madam Premier, it sounds to me like you prefer to keep the public in the dark.

BARKSON
I think the public realizes that most decisions are way too complex for the average brain and best just tucked away and out of the public eye. The last thing we need is for Joe and Jane to get all worked up, worried about forming opinions about issues when their opinion really won't factor into the final decision anyway.

VON ZOOFENDORFEN
So public opinion doesn't factor into your government's decision-making?

BARKSON
Right. Something like that. Correct.

VON ZOOFENDORFEN
Correct?

BARKSON
Correct.

VON ZOOFENDORFEN
Correct?

                    BARKSON
Correct.

                    VON ZOOFENDORFEN
Correct?

                    BARKSON
Correct.

                    VON ZOOFENDORFEN
Yes?

                    BARKSON
Yes.

                    VON ZOOFENDORFEN
Precisely?

                    BARKSON
Precisely.

                    VON ZOOFENDORFEN
Yes?

                    BARKSON
Yes!

                    VON ZOOFENDORFEN
Ha! I know where you're going with this. Nowhere. Do you have anything else you would like to share with the public?

BARKSON
I think everything else is before the courts, so I can't comment on anything, really.

VON ZOOFENDORFEN
Are you sure?

Barkson zips her lips.

BARKSON
Mum's the word.

VON ZOOFENDORFEN
How about final thoughts?

BARKSON
Nah, no initial, middle or final thoughts from this girl.

VON ZOOFENDORFEN
Hardly surprising, but I thought I would ask.

BARKSON
You can always ask.

VON ZOOFENDORFEN
As long as I'm not expecting an answer.

Barkson chuckles.

BARKSON
You will always get an answer.

VON ZOOFENDORFEN
It just might not be informative.

BARKSON
Correct.

VON ZOOFENDORFEN
Correct?

BARKSON
Yes.

Von Zoofendorfen grabs a handkerchief and waves it like a white flag.

VON ZOOFENDORFEN
I know where this is going.

BARKSON
You catch on quick.

VON ZOOFENDORFEN
This has been very enlightening or not, Madam Premier Barkson, and I thank you for your time.

                    BARKSON
          And thank you for helping to
          educate the public.

Von Zoofendorfen looks into camera.

                    VON ZOOFENDORFEN
          There you have it. That's our
          show for today. I'm Francis von
          Zoofendorfen, and you've been
          watching *Pressure Point!*

                    FLOOR DIRECTOR (O.S.)
          And cut.

                    BARKSON
          Are we done?

                    VON ZOOFENDORFEN
          Yes, all done, Madam Premier.

She gets up and stomps off.

                    BARKSON (O.S.)
          Where's my assistant? Alice? I
          thought this was supposed to be
          a campaign fundraiser?

                    VON ZOOFENDORFEN
          Fundraiser? I guess any press
          is good press. Or so they say.

                    BARKSON (O.S.)
              Alice? Where is my assistant?
              How do I get out of here?

A door slams.

                                        FADE TO:

EXT. VANCOUVER SKY (DRONE) — NIGHT

Fireworks explode into the night sky and we
go to . . .

                                        FADE OUT:

                    THE END

Acknowledgements

The *Pressure Point* series was filmed during the COVID-19 crisis, which presented several logistical challenges. In particular, we had to adhere to a number of disease prevention and control protocols, one of which was to reduce the size of the crew and have only six people on the set at any one time. I realized that shooting our program as quickly as possible would reduce the length of time our crew members were exposed to each other, which would also help to reduce the risk of catching and spreading the rapidly mutating virus. The crew was reduced to our director of photography, Athan Merrick, who did triple duty by also being a cameraman and the production designer; two cameramen, Sean Bromley and Peter Planta; one director, me; our host, Patrick Maliha; and our episode guest star. The three-camera shoot allowed us to capture a master and two close-up singles on each take. We also had our two producers, Kyle Toy and Emily Chan, and a hair and make-up artist, Justine Peterson, taking on multiple roles, marshalling in another room, and entering between takes only as needed. This allowed us to film the main interview parts of the series in five days, which meant two episodes per day—so basically, each episode was allocated half a day. It was a challenging and ambitious way to do the show, and I'm grateful to all the cast and crew for their magnificent efforts to wear multiple hats and for pitching in to make it all happen with an extremely small crew.

COVID-19 protocols also meant that we had to keep our splinter units very small for the field reporter segments. These units were structured like an old-school daily news unit with a producer, on-camera reporter, and cameraperson. So, we managed to do them with a maximum of four people present at any one time. A big thanks to Shayan Bayat, Katherine Bransgrove, Grace Chin, Bradley Duffy, Peter Planta, and Kyle Toy not only for doing such a great job with our mini-splinter units but also for making them a lot of fun during an unusually trying time. Also, a big thanks to all the businesses in New Westminster and Burnaby, BC, that allowed me to film in their establishments during the pandemic so I could capture a wide variety of TVs, radios, and monitors to create the opening montages. For those clips, we used a crew of one—me—because more places were receptive to a single person filming rather than a small crew.

A special thanks to Patrick Maliha, our host, who was able to remember and then perform over 120 pages of dialogue in just one week. I'm still in awe of his achievement. And I continue to marvel at his professionalism and ability to pull off such a demanding task with poise and humour throughout the shoot. An amazing performance!

Many thanks, too, to the rest of the interview cast for their wonderful performances: Graem Beddoes, Ryan Cowie, Vivian Davidson, Requell Jodeah, David C. Jones, Sarah Marchand, K.C. Novak, J-C Roy, Zak Santiago, and Alex Zahara. Each one of them brought depth, humour, plenty of accents, and personality to their characters. No one would believe they had been playing their characters for only a few hours.

It was a wonderfully collaborative shoot. I encouraged all the actors to explore and have fun with their characters, so when you see differences between the script and the final show, you're seeing the brilliance of these wonderful actors shining through. Thanks to all of them for making the creation of the series a great experience for me.

Observant viewers of the TV version of *Pressure Point* will no doubt have recognized several voices in the voiceover montages at the beginning of each episode. Cast members stepped in to provide their voices for these montages in what turned out to be a very fun part of the filming process. It was a relatively spontaneous idea on my part, and I'd like to thank them for their flexibility and willingness to participate. On the first day, I was busy writing the lines right on set and handed them the handwritten lines at the end of the first two episodes. After that, I wrote the news montage lines each night for the next day's shoot. There were lots of laughs as we experimented with different voices. A big thanks to all the actors for making the wild line reads a great part of this project.

A great big shout-out to the show's reporters: Shayan Bayat, Katherine Bransgrove, Grace Chin, Bradley Duffy, and Kyle Toy. They had to scramble from one location to another but somehow managed to block out the chaos of our tiny splinter units and deliver wonderfully believable performances which set up the humour to follow in the interviews. Bravo!

Thanks to Sean Bromley for his brilliant edits and work in the opening montage and introduction sequences, which added production values well above our budget. And to Stu Goldberg, who provided perfect, brilliant music in record time. And many thanks to Nathaniel Lyman, my entertainment lawyer, who keeps my writing on the road and not veering off into the liability ditch.

A big thanks to Jan Westendorp for her beautiful design work and help with managing the manuscript through to print. She makes publishing a breeze. And to Lesley Cameron, who is a joy to work with and continues to amaze me with her attention to detail, incredible notes, and story-editing mastery. Thanks as well to Caid Dow, who drafted the book cover in what seemed like minutes and nailed the concept with a simple image of two chairs with a flame under one of them. It says it all.

Finally, a big thanks to my mom. She is my biggest supporter and proudly displays all of my work around her living room for guests to view and read. When I was growing up, there were many heated political debates at family gatherings, and I have often wondered if these comedies are, in part, my way of balancing out our extended family energy from those debates. I hope these comedies will allow us to engage in discussing tough topics with less teeth-clenching and more opening our mouths and hearts to laughter so that we might come together to solve our difficult environmental issues with less conflict. What do you think, Mom?